D0113916

Jeannie C. Riley

From Harper Valley to the Mountain Top

Jeannie C. Riley

From Harper Valley to the Mountain Top

by Jeannie C. Riley
with
Jamie Buckingham

Published by
√chosen books
Lincoln, Virginia 22078

Library of Congress Cataloging in Publication Data

Riley, Jeannie C
   From Harper Valley to the mountain top

   1. Riley, Jeannie C.   2. Country musicians —United States— Biography.   I. Buckingham, Jamie.   II. Title.
ML 420.R567A3   784.5`2`00924   [B]   80-39604
ISBN 0-912376-63-5

Published by
Chosen Books Publishing Company, Ltd.,
Lincoln, Virginia 22078

This book is dedicated...
To Mickey...the other half of me.
To my grandparents, Will and Ada Lee Moore
To my parents, Oscar and Nora Stephenson,
for the precious heritage they gave to me.
Rooted in the gospel truth
and abounding in love,
this heritage,
in turn is my daughter Kim's.

I dedicate this book also to her
and claim for her the promise
which guided me safely home to my Father.

"Train up a child
in the way he should go:
and when he is old
he will not depart from it."
Proverbs 23:6

Acknowledgements

It is with humblest gratitude that I acknowledge my debt to those without whose help this book could never have been published. To Jamie Buckingham for his labor of love, ministring and listening with the heart. To Jackie, Jamie's precious wife, for opening her heart and home to us. To Mickey and Kim for sharing me as I shared our story. To Mama and Daddy for feeding us all as we worked long hours on the book and proving once again that "love is something you do." To Jackie Monaghan, my invaluable assistant, weeping with me as I wept and rejoicing as I rejoiced while I mentally retraced the hills and valleys of my life. To Haskell and Lottie Riley for their constant faith that something good was in process. To my dear sister Helen, and her family—Gene, Lori, and Steve for their love and prayers. To Rev. Stephen and Beckie Niece and the congregation of Franklin (Tennessee) Church of the Nazarene for their constant love and intercessory prayers. To Fuller Arnold for his encouragement. To Laura Watson for her dedication in deciphering the many taped hours of my Texas twang at machine gun speed. And last but not least, to my publishers—Chosen Books— where the entire staff opened their hearts to me and received me as one of them.

Contents

Foreword by Johnny Cash

She was a diamond in the rough, a pretty girl from the little town of Anson, Texas, certain that a brilliant flash in show business was all her heart desired. God gave her worldly success, but more than that, He gave her an awareness of Himself. He chiseled away her rough edges and put a little of His own light in her face. The hand of God clearly shows between the lines in Jeannie C's book.

Her story is a textbook example of what many girls have to come through and will have to go through in order to "make it" in the Nashville music community. Her life speaks of the pitfalls, and she tells the story well.

Her survival through the power of the Holy Spirit and the resulting happiness and rebonding of her marriage are great Bible textbook examples of what the power of God can do in a person's life when that life is receptive to God's commands.

Though she may have been blinded and deluded by her own dreams and ambitions, this maturing Christian woman now has her life in perspective.

In talking to Jeannie C. Riley in person, I get a sense of the Eternal, I discern the joy she knows, and I'm convinced of her Christian integrity by the Spirit within her.

God has polished His diamond in the rough, and that show business flash was just a beginning flicker of the true Light to shine.

Preface

After having written a number of books for others, I told my wife, Jackie, I would never again collaborate with someone on a book. It was too tough—disciplining myself to think like the person whose life I was putting on paper. From now on, I would write only under my own byline.

Then I met Jeannie.

I was hosting a Christian television show, and Jeannie was one of the guests. My writer's instinct immediately set up a whisper campaign.

I tried to resist the idea. However, I did accept Jeannie's invitation to meet her in Kissimmee, Florida, where she was to sing at the Silver Spurs Rodeo. That was only 50 miles from my home in Melbourne. Jackie and I drove over for the evening show.

I was impressed by a girl I knew could sing in any night club in the world but chose to sing at fairs and rodeos, instead, so she could reach "her kind of people."

After the performance, Jackie and I sat in the bedroom of Jeannie's bus, listening as she told us one of the most fascinating stories I had ever heard—the story of her life.

Driving back across the state that night, I realized I needed to relax my self-restriction. Jeannie's story needed to be told.

It took almost three years to complete the project. Of all those I've worked with, no one has touched me as deeply as Jeannie with her honesty and her pain.

I fell in love with the entire family. Mickey Riley is my kind of man. Open. Honest. And in his own way, a real man of God. Kim stole my heart the first time I met her. And Jeannie's folks ... Well, Oscar and Nora Stephenson are the salt of the earth. Besides that, Nora is the best country cook south of the Mason-Dixon line. I became one of the family, enjoying Nora's country sausage and ham, grits, red-eye gravy and homemade biscuits for breakfast in their big farm home outside Nashville.

My first interview with Jeannie set the stage for what was to come. We left her family downstairs in the big antebellum house. Upstairs, on a small balcony overlooking the front yard with towering maples and oaks as our only companions, I explained to Jeannie the mechanics of writing a book.

I warned her I had asked God to give her total recall. I wanted her to be honest enough to give me all the details just as they happened. Those which were not necessary to the book or which would be offensive to her loved ones, would be edited out later. But I asked her to omit nothing as she talked into my tape recorder.

"Good writing," I explained, "is not like painting. There an artist takes an empty canvas, covers it with a wash, paints in the sky and clouds, outlines the mountains and finally places the trees in the foreground.

"The writer," I went on, "is a sculptor. He takes a huge block of marble and chisels away everything that does not look like the story he wants to tell. That's the reason I need for you to tell me everything: every name, every event, every detail. Then together, after it's arranged and typed on paper, we'll chip and chisel."

I could tell she was hesitant. She didn't want to hurt anyone. She didn't want to hurt her parents who had no idea how deeply she had gone into sin. She didn't want to hurt Mickey or Kim or her sister's family. She didn't want to hurt her fans. She didn't even want to hurt those who had hurt her.

"Truth," I told her, "often hurts. But it also heals. I believe God wants to use this book among all those country music fans, not as an exposé, but as an instrument of healing."

Jeannie reached for her ever-present Bible. She let it fall

open on the small white table between us. She began to read where her eyes fell. It was Acts 5, the incredible story of a man and his wife—Ananias and Sapphira—who promised to tell the truth but instead lied to the apostles and dropped dead because of it.

"Thou hast not lied unto men," Peter told Ananias, "but unto God."

Jeannie looked at me, her eyes sparkling. In her Texas drawl she grinned, "I guess that means I better tell the truth and trust God with the rest, doesn't it?"

She never once backed away from that resolve.

To keep from hurting some of the folks Jeannie loves, we have changed the names of several people in the book. In one instance we also changed the details slightly to purposefully disguise a scene. Only those who were involved will recognize what we have done.

But all the rest is true—just as it happened when God picked up the Harper Valley girl and set her on a mountain top.

Jamie Buckingham
Melbourne, Florida

1

A Hot Night in July

I locked the door at Passkey Music Company where I worked as a secretary and headed down the street. It was a hot, humid evening. A few blocks away was Ryman Auditorium, the home of Nashville's Grand Ole Opry, with its dark red bricks and big white windows looking for all the world like the temple it is.

I had longed to sing there ever since I was a little girl in West Texas. I had yearned to be there with country singing stars Ernest Tubb, Roy Acuff, Kitty Wells and Loretta Lynn, listening to the pickin' and twangin' and waiting for my turn to come on stage.

Instead, for two years I had walked the streets of Nashville with my little demo tape, hoping someone would come along and turn me into a star. Nothing had come of it.

I turned into Columbia Studio where Shelby Singleton and his group of musicians were waiting for me. My friends had set me up for this one. They had intimidated me into signing a contract with Plantation Records. That night I was supposed to record a song about small town hypocrisy. I didn't like it. It didn't seem right for me at all. I wanted to sing country music—not cheap pop. Besides, they wanted me to record it under another name. Even my identity was about to be obliterated.

On this hot, humid July evening in 1968, the entire nation was in turmoil. Men were being killed in Vietnam and no one really knew why.

College students were demonstrating on the campuses.

There had been riots in Detroit and Watts.

My marriage was heading for the rocks.

I was angry and confused.

I was a small-town girl from Anson, Texas, who had been swallowed alive by music City.

Shelby met me in the studio and introduced me to the musicians. He had a copy of the music in his hand. "It's just right for your voice," he said. "Tom Hall has caught the angry mood of the country. Let's see if you can make it sing."

I had already studied the words. I looked them over again resentfully and leaned into the mike. The guitars began strummin' and the dobro was going "dwoang, dwoang . . ."

Suddenly I was into the song. It caught me hard like it was to catch the entire nation:

> I want to tell you all a story about a Harper Valley widowed wife
> Who had a teenage daughter who attended Harper Valley Junior High
> Well, her daughter came home one afternoon and didn't stop to play,
> And she said, "Mom, I've got a note here from the Harper Valley PTA . . ."

2

Dream Big

My earliest memory of Anson, Texas, is living in a house that had no foundation under it. All we had was a little frame box that sat on concrete-block pillars. The hot, west-Texas wind blew under it in the summer, and the blue northers whined and moaned around it in the winter when we nearly froze to death.

I remember vowing that some day, somehow, some way, I was going to taste the excitement promised by the world outside of Anson. I was going to be somebody. Somebody big. The world was going to know that Jeannie Stephenson was a special person.

I grew up lonely. My sister Helen was five grades ahead of me. Competition was a way of life as I determined early to measure up to her and the standards set by others. When a school friend came home with me in the third grade and made fun of my house, it hurt.

"My house is prettier than yours," she sniped. "You live in a house on stilts. We have a foundation."

So I dreamed of a house with a foundation—one you couldn't see under, where the neighborhood dogs didn't lie, where all the pipes from the plumbing didn't show, and where you couldn't hear it half a block away when someone flushed the toilet.

The next year, when we moved into our new home, I could hardly wait to ask my friend to come home with me after school and show her our new house—the one with the solid foundation. She was impressed.

"Oh, your house is pretty," she said softly. "But," she added quickly, "my mother is prettier than yours."

I wanted to scream. I couldn't go out and get a new mother like we did a new house. Besides, I loved my mother, even if she was a plain-looking housewife.

Mama was always a country girl. Her father, whom everyone called "Brother Moore," was a Nazarene minister. They had always been poor, but Mama said the Lord had always provided just the things they needed. And somehow Mama never seemed to need much. She made her own clothes out of feed sacks. She made ours—Helen's and mine—out of the same thing. Except for Easter. Every year she made beautiful, frilly dresses with lace and ruffles for Helen and me, working on them for weeks ahead of time. It didn't bother me at the time that we always had beautiful dresses for Easter while Mama wore an old feed sack dress to church. In those days Mama still had a lot of the old Nazarene ways in her even though we went to the Baptist church. Plain dresses. No makeup. Always working, at home, in the cotton fields or at the hospital as a nurse.

One day I uttered my first real prayer—that I would make it big as a singer in Nashville; then I would send for my mama and papa and let them move into my mansion. I'd help her get new teeth and teach her how to fix her hair and wear fancy dresses. And when I stood on the stage at the Grand Ole Opry and got my awards for the best country singer in the nation, Mama would be there in the front row, dressed in a beautiful evening dress, her face a-beaming with joy. Then I'd be able to say to my friend, "See, my mama *is* prettier than yours."

Other girls in Anson helped with knitting, sewing and cooking, but I spent all my spare time memorizing country music. I had taken shorthand in high school for just that one purpose: copying the words of the songs as I heard them on the radio. Then I'd write them over in longhand and sing them over and over. By the time I was 16 I had learned more than 400 country songs by heart, singing them without the accompaniment of any instruments.

Daddy never did say much around the house. Raised on a farm in West Texas where the only thing deeper than the dust in summer were the snow drifts in winter, he worked hard as an automobile mechanic. Although he had not gone to school much, I knew he was a wise man even before I knew what wisdom was. Somehow he seemed to grasp situations and come up with the right answers. But he had a problem with his 16-year-old daughter.

By the time I was a sophomore in high school, the war inside me was raging fierce. Maybe it was a reflection of the mood of the nation in the early '60s. The Korean War was over, there was a crisis in Berlin and talk of more trouble in a place called Vietnam. When my boyfriend, Mickey Riley, had graduated from high school and had been called to active duty in the navy, I was ready to leave home. But how? How does a 16-year-old girl just pick up and leave a little town of 2,000?

My uncle, Johnny Moore, played the guitar in a country music band. Ever since he had gone to Nashville with some musicians to do recordings, everybody in Anson considered him something of a star. I mean, after all, how many folks from Anson had ever been to Nashville?

It was Uncle Johnny who arranged for me to sing at the Jones County Jamboree held once a month at an old schoolhouse in Truby, about a 20-minute ride from Anson. It was winter, and the wind was making almost as much noise outside as the string band in the old auditorium. I wore a pair of gold, wool slacks and a matching wool sweater. Mama was working the 3-to-11 shift at the hospital, but Daddy was there to hear me.

I was nervous. My heart was pounding. When they called me to the microphone, though, I belted out two songs in perfect meter and didn't forget a single word. I knew there would be a next time. And that the next time would be easier. I was on my way.

That night Daddy bragged about me to Mama. "Jeannie sang tonight," he said when Mama got home from the hospital. "I was proud of the little booger. She done real good."

I lay awake most of the night listening to the wind beat the limbs of an old tree against the side of the house and wishing Mickey had been there to hear me instead of being way off in Iceland in the navy. Already I was planning what I would sing the next month at the jamboree.

Mickey returned from the navy as I began my senior year in high school in the fall of 1962. Right away he started talking about marriage. I knew he was right for me and began dreaming about becoming a married woman. We had gone together for more than three years. He had a good job with the highway department which paid $180 a month. I had turned 18 that October and wanted to go ahead and finish high school. All I had to do was move out of Daddy's house into an apartment with Mickey. So Mickey agreed to come over and ask my folks if he could marry me—which was the custom in Anson unless it was a shotgun wedding.

We were all sitting at the kitchen table when Mickey came in the next night. He looked awful thin, dressed in jeans, cowboy boots and straw hat. But I was too excited to think about how he looked or the fact that while the Stephenson family was poor, moving in with Mickey meant he and I would be even poorer.

In our family everything was always done around the kitchen table. We might as well not have had a living room. We didn't watch TV as a family; we never gathered as a family except at the supper table. Mickey arrived while Mama was taking the dirty dishes off the table and Daddy was leaning back in his chair with a toothpick.

Mickey made it short and said we wanted to be married on December 20. Daddy listened, nodded, cleared his throat and said, "Well, I'm going to bed."

"Oh, you're not leaving me here with this, are you?" Mama said anxiously, looking to me and then at Mickey.

"Yes," Daddy said as he stood up. "The girl's turned 18, and I've been expecting it. I figure they are going to do what they're going to do, so I'm going to bed."

Halfway through the door he turned and looked at Mickey. "All I can say to you, young man, is, you be good to her. Because if you ain't, I'll have her right back here with me."

Mickey swallowed, nodded and blinked behind his glasses. "I'll be good to her, Oscar," he stammered. "Me and Jeannie, we gonna do fine."

Daddy nodded and headed toward the bedroom.

"Can't you wait until next June?" Mama cried softly. "I wanted you to finish high school."

"Now, Mama," I said, "we'll stay here until I finish high school. Then we'll be moving to Nashville."

"That's right," Mickey said. "Jeannie's going to the top as a singer. Just you wait."

But Mama wasn't able to walk into our dream and see all the wonderful things we could see. She sat at the supper table, crying. I cleared the dishes and straightened up the kitchen trying to make her feel better, but the shock was too much for her.

"We've already lost Helen," Mama sobbed. Four years before, my sister had married Gene Scott who worked in the local bank. Now she was busy having babies.

Mama finally got up and headed to bed. Mickey and I stood on the front door stoop for a few minutes. He was nervous, shaking. "It's okay," I told him. "Mama's always like that. She gives out like a dog that has a terrible bite; then she'll whimper awhile and be all right. In fact, I'll bet anything she'll start making out an invitation list right away."

I went to bed that night with an excited feeling. My wedding date was set. Then my thoughts were disturbed by the little streak of yellow light coming from under the bathroom door. I knew Mama was in there and wondered what she was doing, staying so long. Anxious thoughts came into my mind. I got out of bed and went to the bathroom, gently opening the door. There she sat on the side of the tub with the little Anson, Texas, phone book in her lap. She had a notebook laid out on the toilet seat and was making out an invitation list. She had started with the "A" section, jotting down names of all our friends who might come to the wedding, and had already gotten to "P" when I came in. Bless her! She knew I wasn't an organizer, and if the wedding was going to be worth a flip, she would have to do it. So there she was at midnight sitting in the bathroom making out the invitation list.

Mickey and I were married in the Baptist Church. One of my dreams had come true. Now for the biggest one — Nashville.

3

The Promise

Mickey and I moved into a small apartment and struggled each month to make it on his salary. We postponed going to Nashville until I graduated from high school and we could save some money.

I was at the doctor's office for a check-up when he told me he thought I was pregnant. "In another month we'll know for sure," he said.

"Can't you find out sooner?" I asked, excited.

"Yes, I can run a test and let you know this afternoon. But it will cost another $5, and you young folks. . ."

"Give me the test," I interrupted. "I don't think I can stand to wait."

That night I could hardly wait for Mickey to get home. "We're gonna have a baby," I shouted when he walked in the door. He grabbed my hands, and we danced all over the house. Then we rushed out to the car and drove all over town telling anyone who would listen.

Kim was born January 11, 1966. Mickey and I were happier that year than we had ever been.

During this time I became close to my sister Helen and her husband, Gene Scott. Their two older children, Lori and Steve, were as precious to me as they were to Helen. But it was the little baby, Bryan, toddling around on tiny little legs, who completely won everyone's heart.

Mickey and I were having lunch at the Sirloin Cafe one day when a friend burst in the door. She had ridden all over town (which couldn't have taken more than five minutes in Anson) to find us.

"Jeannie, come to the hospital, quick. It's Bryan. His temperature is 106 degrees, and they've packed him in ice."

The first person I saw at the hospital was Mama. She was running down the hall wringing her hands. People were running along beside her, trying to comfort her.

I thought the baby had already died, and I began to cry. Then a nurse told us that Bryan had encephalitis and meningitis, a combination which was almost always fatal. The diseases had come from a mosquito bite.

How could anything as small as a mosquito suddenly take the life from a living, breathing, laughing baby? My emotions ran in all directions. Hate for the mosquito. Terror that Bryan might die. Guilt that I had done something wrong for which God was punishing us all.

I grabbed Aunt Ollie, Mama's sister, and said, "Aunt Ollie, it's all my fault. Will you go and pray with me?"

She told me firmly that it was not my fault, but the two of us went into the ladies room and got on our knees. The only real prayer I had ever uttered before was that God would make it possible for me to go to Nashville and become a superstar. Now that I needed to talk to Him in a very serious way, I realized I didn't even know who He was.

My relationship with God had been limited to joining the Baptist church and being baptized. I had submitted to immersion simply because all the other kids had done the same during a late summer revival. I felt there was a God. And I said that I believed Jesus was His Son, whatever that meant. But I also felt that God had some kind of claim on me and would surely punish me for all my sins. So it was with a lot of fear that I knelt there with Aunt Ollie on the asphalt tile floor of the ladies room, weeping and begging God not to take little Bryan.

At that moment I decided I needed to give up something. Surely God would demand things from folks to see if they were really serious. I remembered the Old Testament stories of the animal sacrifices, how Abraham had even been willing to sacrifice his son Isaac to God. But what did I have that I could give Him? I would have given my life for little Bryan, if I felt that would have saved him.

Suddenly it occurred to me that I should give up my singing career—a career which was still nothing more than a dream. But it was terribly important to me. So I began to pray.

"Lord, I won't ever sing again. I won't go to Nashville. I won't try to be a star."

Surely now that I had given God all this, He would do something for that little baby back there in the hospital room.

I rose from my knees feeling that Bryan was going to get well. I didn't know anything about miracles. But surely if someone was as sincere as I was in willing to forfeit her whole life, then God would give a life back in return. I went back to Bryan's room and told Gene and Helen, "Bryan's going to be all right."

"I wish the Lord would tell me that," Helen said.

Day after day Bryan lay in bed semi-conscious, unable to recognize anyone. My guilt returned, and I began repeating my promise to God on a daily basis. One day I drove out to the county dump in our old car and leaned over the fender, praying. "I won't try to be a star," I told Him. "I'll even join the Holiness Church if You want me to. I'll wipe off all my lipstick and never sing another country song."

Somehow being at the dump seemed appropriate, like I deserved to be out there with all the garbage.

That afternoon, when I returned to the hospital, Bryan opened his eyes for the first time. The next day he was able to get out of bed and walk a little bit, holding onto his mommy's hands. Helen cried and said she knew God had saved him so he could be a preacher or a heart surgeon. It was a miracle.

When Bryan was back at home and almost fully recovered, the thought came: *Maybe I was hasty in that restroom, down on my knees wailing with Aunt Ollie. Maybe little Bryan would have gotten well without my prayers.*

The desire to sing country music again and to go to Nashville had returned strong. But to do so I would have to turn from God. I should have gone to our preacher to sort this out, but I tried to do it myself.

Was Bryan's healing from God or not? Maybe it could have come without Him. Maybe there wasn't any God. Or, if there was, maybe He really didn't care what I did. I mean, He didn't seem to stop me when I did other things wrong.

If I wanted to sing so much and it was wrong, wouldn't He reach down and stop me? I mean, if I was God and my children did things I didn't want them to do, that's how I would handle it. I finally concluded that there was a God, but He really didn't care what I did. After all, I was only one girl in a world of billions of people.

Then a letter arrived from Weldon Myrick. Weldon had played the steel guitar at the Jones County Jamboree at Truby School and had heard me sing.

Now he had gone to work for Bill Anderson in Nashville. Bill had discovered a little housewife in Ohio whose first record went straight to the top. Her name was Connie Smith, and she was number one in the nation. Weldon said that every time he heard Connie Smith sing "Once a Day" he thought of me. He said we even looked alike since she had long hair.

I had heard Connie Smith sing. Anyone listening to country music on the radio knew about her. But I didn't know that Weldon was working for Bill Anderson or that Bill was the one who had discovered Connie.

Suddenly a bright hope reappeared in my dreams. The dream of Nashville was alive again. I bought a copy of *Country Song Roundup,* with a picture of Connie Smith on the cover, at the drugstore. Then I bought Connie's "Once a Day" and played it over and over. I sang along with her on the record. She had a little loop in her voice where she'd sort of pop it at the end of a line. So I put a little pop in my voice. There were certain ways she delivered certain words—with a shove. I was already doing that, but I accented it even more. I even raised my voice a half key to sing where she sang—not realizing the strain would cause me to sing flat for years to come.

I would listen to the Grand Ole Opry on Saturday night radio and cry. Oh, to be on that wonderful show with Connie Smith, Loretta Lynn and all the other superstars. I'd be washing dishes in my kitchen and listening to Merle Haggard singing "Swinging Doors," and my tears would fall in the dishwater. I would be giving Kim her bottle, and the music from the radio would switch me a thousand miles away. The fragrance of stardom scented every evening breeze, beckoning me to faraway Nashville.

4

Music City

*I*t was my uncle, Johnny Moore, who helped me reach for my star. Uncle Johnny had cut a few records, all small-time stuff. One of his songs, "Fifteen Acres of Peanut Land," had been featured in *Billboard* magazine as the spotlight pick of the week. But Uncle Johnny never had been able to get the necessary backing to make his songs go over. He'd make a trip to Nashville, cut a record in a little studio and then bring it back to Anson. But he was too busy running his service stations to promote his records. So they got lost.

But he had been to Nashville several times. And he did know the music business. So when he suggested that we all accompany him on one of his trips to Music City to cut another record, it was the chance of a lifetime.

Mickey and I didn't have a car that would make the trip—and everybody knew that you didn't dare go to Nashville unless you were driving a Cadillac. So Uncle Johnny borrowed another Cadillac to pair with his, and 13 of us piled into the two cars and set out for Nashville. Uncle Johnny, his wife and four children rode in one car. Mickey drove the other car with me, Kim, Mama and Daddy and Mickey's parents. We looked a mess, driving over to Dallas and then up through Arkansas to Memphis and on to Nash-

ville. But when you're swinging on a star, you don't care
what the rope looks like.

Driving into Nashville in a Cadillac was like riding into
heaven. Riding down Broadway there was Hewgley's Record
Shop and Tootsie's Orchid Lounge. Music poured from open
doors and out onto the streets. There were posters of stars
in all the windows. Down the street was Ernest Tubb's
Record Shop. I had heard the Ernest Tubb Record Shop
program on late Saturday-night radio.

"Look at that," Mickey said, pointing out the car window.
There in front of Ernest Tubb's was an old drunk, leaning
on a parking meter and singing into it as though it were
a microphone. "I guess they don't all make it, do they?"
Mickey said.

Then we rounded a corner and right in front us was the
throne room of music heaven—Ryman Auditorium, the home
of the Grand Ole Opry. Its old red brick was accented by
the white frames around the huge cathedral windows. I just
sat there in the car and cried.

That very night Uncle Johnny got us into the Opry. He
had been there a number of times before and knew the
guards at the door. Mickey's mother and daddy and Johnny's
wife and kids stayed at the motel, but the rest of us all got
in. I could hardly believe it, but we were actually backstage
at the Opry.

We stood on one side and watched the stars enter. The
door opened and there was Loretta Lynn, wearing simple
old blue jeans and carrying a big purse over one arm. She
had one of her little twins by the hand and was holding
the other in her arm. Her hair was up in rollers. Within
minutes her hair was fixed, and she was on stage singing
the number one song in the nation, "You Ain't Woman
Enough to Take My Man."

Then there was little Connie Smith. *I know her better
than she knows herself,* I thought. I could sing every one
of her songs just like she did them. As she waited backstage
to go on at the Grand Ole Opry, I pulled my autograph
book out of my purse and fearfully made my way over to
her.

"Oh, would it be too much trouble for you to sign an

autograph for my little niece?" I asked. I was afraid to ask
for myself. But I had taught little Lori "Once a Day," and
she loved Connie as I did.

"What's her name?" Connie asked, taking the autograph
book and pen.

I was thrilled she asked. She put, "To Lori, best wishes
always, sincerely, Connie Smith."

All the biggies were there that night: Roy Acuff, the dean
of country music; and Porter Wagoner with his sequined
suit; Chet Atkins, who could make a guitar sing like an
angel, played a couple of songs. He was the number one
instrumentalist in the nation at the time. I loved their music,
but they weren't the competition. The women were the competition, and inside I kept saying to myself as the women
breezed on and off stage, *You don't know it, but you're
passing right by the girl who is going to take this town
and turn it upside down. One day they're going to be crowd-
ing around and asking me for autographs. And they'll be
out there, clapping and shouting and whistling and demanding encores from me.*

It was June 1966. And I was 22 years old.

Uncle Johnny introduced me to a lot of folks that night,
and I followed him around like a little puppy dog, grinning
and sparkling, trying not to act too country. But it was the
biggest night of my life to date, and there was no way to
hide my excitement.

One of the fellows who made a special effort to talk to
me that night was Jackie Phelps, who later went on to play
guitar on the television show "Hee-Haw." Cute, with a little
dimple in his chin, Jackie told Uncle Johnny he wanted to
talk to me. But I was so starry-eyed that he pulled Uncle
Johnny aside instead.

Later that night Uncle Johnny told me what Jackie Phelps
had said: "Your little niece is a pretty country girl, and I'd
like to save her and her husband some heartache. If she's
got talent, tell her she doesn't have to sell her body to make
it to the top. She can make it if she knows the right people.
But if she gets in with the wrong crowd, they'll destroy
her—and her home too."

I giggled when Uncle Johnny told me. I didn't see any

"wrong" people. They were all right as far as I could see, dressed in their glittering outfits, laughing, smiling, signing autographs, waving at the crowd and belting out wonderful music.

Uncle Johnny was never one to push things—the reason he hadn't made it bigger with his records. So I was surprised when he reached out and grabbed a man named Doyle Wilburn by the arm backstage that evening. The Wilburn Brothers, Doyle and Teddy, were part of a family of brothers who had started by singing in churches and later made it to the big time at the Opry. They had their own TV show and publishing business—Sure-Fire Music. It was common talk they were the ones who had made a star out of Loretta Lynn since she was the vocalist on their TV show. Now they had their own booking agency as well.

"Doyle, I don't mean to bug you, but I got my little niece here." Wilburn stopped and turned, smiling.

"If you would just listen to her sing one time, I know you'd be interested. I think she's got it."

I knew Uncle Johnny would never have done that for himself. He did it just for me, because I was his sister's baby girl.

I expected Doyle to pull away, shaking his head. He must have 20 such requests each evening. But because he liked Uncle Johnny, he responded.

"Well, how long will you be here?" he asked Uncle Johnny, his eyes on me.

"Long enough," Uncle Johnny almost shouted.

"Okay. If you could bring her by the office, say about Wednesday, we'll give her a listen."

My heart never stopped pounding between then and Wednesday. I was going to have a chance to audition. The Wilburn brothers' office for Sure-Fire Music was in an old two-story house on 16th Avenue South. Mickey, Uncle Johnny and Mama went with me.

The secretary introduced me to Johnny Russell, who at that time was working with the Wilburns before he became a country music entertainer himself. He looked like a teddy bear. Black-headed, short, roly-poly. In fact, he was huge. He joked he had to have his boots specially made because his calves were so big. "There may be a lot of good singers around Nashville," he laughed as he took us back into the recording room in the middle of the house, "but none of 'em's big enough to fill these boots."

The room was big, without windows. There was a long desk with all sorts of tapes and sound equipment. It looked real official, very impressive. We had no sooner gotten seated than the phone rang. It was Brenda Lee calling for Johnny. I could hardly believe it. Brenda was the big crossover star at the time, having been one of the first to make the switch from country music into pop. She was asking Johnny about a Loretta Lynn song she wanted to sing.

"Wow," I whispered to Mickey, "they're really in touch here."

Johnny Russell played me a couple of cuts from Loretta Lynn's latest album, then he asked my Uncle Johnny to accompany me for a couple of stock songs. He listened and made no comment. Then he asked if I did any writing. I sang him two or three of mine. The last one, called, "It's Our Anniversary and You're Not Mine," was too much for him. He broke out laughing in the middle of the song. When I finished he said, "Ah—Jeannie—I think we can just shelve that one."

But there was one song he was interested in, one I called "Lonely Just Walked In." He said they would like to record and publish it. He asked if that was all right with me.

I looked at Mickey, then Uncle Johnny. Both were beaming. "Sure! Gracious, yes!" After all, that's what I was there for.

Johnny Russell excused himself to go in the other room and talk to Doyle Wilburn. I overheard snatches of their conversation.

"Work with her, Johnny . . . she's a little bit too much like Connie Smith . . . probably been memorizing her stuff . . . she drives everything home, too, like Connie . . . needs to perfect her own style."

That was the day I learned I had to have a style of my own to get anywhere. Loretta Lynn has feeling. From the day she hit Nashville, she felt everything she sang. It was her style. Connie is a driver. She pushes her voice and accents with it. She has a big, pow-pow delivery. I realized if I was going to make it big, I would have to do it as Jeannie Riley, not as another Connie Smith.

"You can learn a lot from Loretta," Johnny Russell said as we talked in the recording studio. "She's never quit learning. She listens to people. She still takes advice. She relies on Teddy Wilburn's advice. In fact, if they book her into the studio and Teddy is out on the road, she makes them wait until he is back."

Arrangements were made for Uncle Johnny to take me out to Bradley's Barn that night. Bradley's Barn was just what it sounds like—a big, old barn about 25 minutes outside Nashville, which had become a famous recording studio and which was later destroyed by fire.

I had lost down to 105 pounds after Kim was born and felt petite and glamorous—ready to be a star. I dressed up in my little orange dress that had yellow and blue ruffles on the skirt and a yellow bow at the top with a big scoop neck. Yellow shoes and a yellow handbag completed my outfit. I didn't know that all I was doing was cutting some demonstration tapes for their publishing company. From thousands of these demo tapes several hundred records might be made of which very few would be hits.

I recorded two songs that first night and two more the next night. The following day I was at the TV taping of the Wilburn Brothers show. A photographer from WSM came on the set to make pictures of me. I could hardly believe all that was happening. Already I was center stage. I kept glancing over at Mickey who was dressed in his jeans, boots and cowboy hat, standing over in the shadows. Was he as thrilled as I was?

The following night Mickey and I were back in the motel watching a famous singer on television. I snuggled up to Mickey on the sofa and pointed an accusing finger at the woman on the screen: "How could you have the nerve to sing on national TV? You've divorced your second husband and are living with another man."

Mickey was quiet, his eyes closed behind his glasses. "Don't be too hard on her. You don't know everything that's gone on."

"It makes no difference," I shot back. "She has no right

to appear on TV when her life's all messed up like that. Believe you me, when I make it to the top, nothing will be able to come between us."

I reached for Mickey's hand, but he was getting up to go to the bathroom where he had an ice chest filled with beer. I leaned back on the sofa and shook my head disapprovingly at the television set. The next day after more recording at Bradley's Barn, Johnny Russell pulled Mickey and me aside.

"I've watched you kids ever since you got here, and I need to say something to you. Nashville is good to you when you're on top. But it's a mean city, too. This business of wanting to be number one gets in your blood. It consumes you until you can't think of anything else. It's like drugs, only worse, 'cause there's nothing you can do to get rid of it. You'll leave your family. You'll leave your self-respect. You'll do anything to reach the top—and anything to stay there. I've seen it happen too many times. Most people think they are the exception. They come in here with high morals and high ideals—and lose them overnight. The pressures are too much. What I'm saying is this: I don't think Jeannie can make it here. She's got a good voice, and you're a fine young couple. But this city will chew you up, swallow the juice and spit you out like a dry hull on the street. Go back to Texas. And stay there."

Mickey never commented on what Johnny said. He just listened, thanked him, and then we returned to the motel. That night I lay awake nearly all night long, thinking. There on the dresser was a reel of tape which contained my voice singing four songs with a real, live Nashville band behind me. That was the beginning. I was going to make it big. I was going to have a big bus that would take me and my band all over the nation.

I lay there, staring up into the darkness, remembering my daddy playing me to sleep at night with the harmonica as we sat around late in our house in Texas. I loved the sound of what he called "nigger blues," that soft wail of the French harp moaning through the night. It's the same sound I had heard out at Bradley's Barn when they had recorded my songs. I could just see myself standing on a stage, singing with the wild harmonica wailing in the background.

Ten days later we left to return to Anson. Doyle Wilburn had talked with Uncle Johnny and said they had a tour of Germany coming up in September. They needed a girl vocalist to go along and would be contacting me.

July passed. Then August. I couldn't think of anything but Nashville. But the Wilburns had not contacted me about their Germany tour in September. I was confused.

One afternoon Mickey came in from work and said, "Start packing your stuff. I've quit my job. We're moving to Nashville. I'm tired of seeing you mope around. If we're ever going to try it, it might as well be now while we're still young."

I could hardly believe it. I was scared. But exhilarated. In less than two weeks we were ready to move.

The day we left everyone came to see us off: Mama and Daddy, Helen, Gene and their kids who were like my very own, Uncle Johnny, Aunt Sue and their kids. We were all crying. It was as if pieces of my heart were being torn out and left behind. Our family was so close, and I was the first to ever move away.

We had a big U-Haul trailer hooked onto the back of our 1957 Chevrolet. Everything we owned was crammed inside. Kim was asleep on the back seat. We said our last good-bys and Mickey pointed us toward Music City. As the brown part of Texas dropped behind us and we moved into the green areas north and east of Dallas, we began to talk about the future.

I could almost feel the round piece of pressed wax in my hand with my name on the label. Capitol. Decca. Columbia. RCA. Connie was on RCA. That was the one I wanted.

"I love the way that little dog looks down that megaphone," I told Mickey. "You know what it says? 'His master's voice.' I want to be the master. Then they'll listen to me."

As we drove into the city limits of Nashville, Mickey and I made a pact that we'd always travel together as a family. Little Kim would go with us too. Show business might chew up other folks and spit them out on the sidewalk, but not us. We'd show 'em.

We were going to make it. Together.

5

The Promised Land

It was Indian summer when we arrived. The nights were soft with haze in the air. The trees along the boulevards of Nashville stood like winged angels protecting the people of this heavenly place. Romance was in the atmosphere. In the late twilight Mickey would take us for rides around the city. In Texas everything was flat, but here there were hills. And trees. Thousands of them, their leaves just beginning to turn color in the early autumn.

I especially loved the old antebellum mansions. I could picture myself standing on the brick walk coming down from the big porch with the white pillars. Dressed in a ruffled organdy dress, my hair falling down my back and a big magnolia blossom pinned my shoulder. Texas and the house on stilts were all behind me. After I made it big, I was going to bring my daddy and mama to live with us in our Nashville mansion. Mickey would travel with me as my companion and business manager. Little Kim would sit in the front of the bus and talk to the driver and kid with my band. I would have a private suite in the back of the bus where I'd sit, write notes to my fans and watch the nation smile and wave as we passed.

Back in Anson everything seemed so small. But here even the shanties had an air of distinction. The old railway station, its stone smoky gray and its windows covered with the dust of 10,000 trains rumbling through the city, was special to me. It signified travel.

The first two weeks we were in Nashville we lived in the Tennessee Motel. Mickey had a job running a service station Uncle Johnny had bought shortly before we arrived. It was Uncle Johnny's investment so we could all survive in Nashville. He felt if I made it, we could help him make it, too.

But it wasn't that easy. I wondered why I had never heard from Doyle Wilburn, especially since I had written him and told him we were moving to Nashville, and he could contact me in care of the Tennessee Motel. It never occurred to me that the Wilburns probably interviewed eight or ten singers a month just like me and forgot most of them in a matter of days.

I finally made a trip down to Sure-Fire Music to see Doyle Wilburn. He wasn't in and nobody there could even remember my name. But the secretary said she would have someone call me. No one did.

I finally got a man on the phone who said he was a "musical director" for Sure-Fire Music. He told me I wasn't needed since the Germany trip had been cancelled. "Go out and get some experience and call us back," he said tersely.

Get experience? How could I do that when all I had was one little demo tape which I carried around in my purse? Why had they shown so much interest in me? Why the photographer?

Mickey rented us a small efficiency apartment in Madison, a suburb of Nashville. It was the next to last house on the street—Cherry Street—which came to a dead end in a swamp. There was something depressing, almost symbolic, about this dead-end street. I was homesick for Mama and Daddy. Mama had always taken care of me. Even after I was married I would go to Mama's, and she would roll my hair. Now I was alone—and had to do it myself.

Mickey soon was working 12 hours a day—seven days a week—at the service station. He had made a copy of my tape and played it to his customers. But nothing seemed to help. I missed my sister. I missed her children.

But the dream never faded. I believed that every time I went to the mailbox there would be a letter waiting which would be my doorway to stardom. When the doorbell rang, my heart would leap in my throat, hoping it was someone from Music Row asking me to come on down and cut the next big record.

But the doorbell never rang. The only letters in the mailbox were from my family in Anson. It was bad enough living on a dead-end street. But a street that dead-ended into a swamp was worse. I begged Mickey to find us a bigger apartment, closer to his work.

Weeks of waiting produced nothing. Winter was approaching and the leaves were beginning to fall. I had to do something. One morning I took Mickey to work and returned to our house with the car. I fixed my hair the best I could, picked up my tape, put Kim in our car and headed for Music Row.

Marijohn Wilkin was the only name I knew in Nashville who might be helpful to me. Marijohn was from Merkel, Texas, about 25 miles from Anson. She was a successful songwriter and owned Buckhorn Music Publishing Company and the well-known Marijohn Singers. I knew she had never heard of me, but since she was from my section of Texas, I thought she might, as a favor, listen to my tape. The little reel, in its small box, rested on the seat between me and the baby, Kim, who was strapped in her infant seat.

All I knew was that Marijohn's office was some place on 16th Avenue South in downtown Nashville. But I couldn't find it. I drove up and down the unfamiliar street looking at the signs over the offices. I finally backed into a parking slot next to a meter, dropped in a dime and returned to the car. I bottle-fed seven-months-old Kim in the front seat, then, picking up my tape, cradled Kim in my arm and started walking.

I went into three or four places asking questions, looking for Marijohn, hoping to run into somebody who might help. It was as if I were propelled by some kind of force.

Around noon I finally walked into the office of Chart Records. My feet hurt. Kim was getting heavier and heavier. I was sweating profusely in the hot, midday sun. I asked the man at the front desk if he knew where Marijohn Wilkin's office was.

He looked up from his papers. He was young, slender.

"Why, you got a tape?" he asked.

I didn't know at the time how carefully music company employees avoided aspiring singers who walked in off the street with demo tapes. But for some reason this fellow seemed to feel sorry for me.

"I'm from Anson," I said, as if everyone in the world knew where Anson was.

He gave me a puzzled look.

I blushed. "I mean Anson, Texas. It's just a few miles from where Marijohn is from. I thought she might be interested in hearing me sing."

He puffed his cheeks and blew out—slowly, expressing discomfort.

I just stood there, looking at him. Kim began to wiggle. I shifted her to the other arm but never took my eyes off his face.

"I don't know where to go," I said honestly. "I don't want to bother anybody, but I just gotta be a singer."

He returned my stare. Maybe he'd never heard anyone talk that way. Maybe he really believed me. His eyes dropped, and he pushed the drawer of his desk closed, turned a key to lock it and stood up. "Okay," he said, shaking his head. "Bring your tape, and I'll give it a listen."

He took me down a hall and into a studio. Putting the tape on the machine, he sat down with a resigned look. There was my voice again. The same voice singing the same songs I had listened to a hundred times since they were made out at Bradley's Barn. I was afraid to watch his face as he listened. Fearful of what I might see. I just sat down in the little hard-backed chair and looked at the floor. Waiting.

"Not bad," he mused. "Not bad at all." He rewound the tape and played it through again. My heart was in my throat. This time I watched his face and could tell he was impressed. "You know we've just come out with Lynn Anderson doing 'Ride, Ride, Ride.' It's gonna be a biggie for sure. But you've got something on the ball, too. Let me get my boss."

I was too nervous to even swallow. All I could do was gulp. I sat straight in the little chair, my feet and knees together, Kim on my lap, waiting. The head man bustled into the room and stood at the door as the younger man rewound the tape and cut on the big speakers. My voice filled the room.

"Too much like Loretta Lynn," the head man snorted. He turned and walked out.

The young man turned and looked at me. "Sorry," he shrugged, "he's the boss. I just work here."

He rewound the tape, carefully put it in the box and handed it to me. "Maybe you're not supposed to be here," he said gently. "There's a lot of girls who come to Nashville who have far better voices than any of the big Opry stars. I mean, they can sing circles around them. But it's not the voice. It's not even the song. It's what we call in Nashville 'the breaks.' You've gotta be at the right place at the right time with the right song and the right voice. Maybe you ought to head back to Anson and just forget about Nashville. There's too many girls just like you here already."

I took the tape and dropped it in my purse. It didn't change a thing. I knew I was going to make it, even though I felt my heart sink.

The man reached out and touched my hand. His eyes were sad, and this time he didn't drop his gaze. It was as though he could see the future in my eyes and wanted to comfort me. He started to speak but instead withdrew his hand and shrugged.

I thanked him, walked out the door onto the street and toward my car. It wasn't until I got in the front seat that I began to cry.

It was early afternoon when I pulled up in front of Mickey's Texaco station on Dickerson Road. Kim was asleep in her baby seat, her head leaning far over to one side. I was sweating from struggling with the big steering wheel on the old Chevy. My hair was hanging across my face like strings from a wet mop. My mascara had run until it was gone. I was too tired even to care any longer.

Mickey came to the car window on my side. A good looking young man, a few years older, was beside him. Tall, big, with a flat-top haircut. "Jerry, this is my wife, Jeannie," Mickey said. "Jeannie, this is Jerry Chesnut."

Before anything else was said, Jerry looked in through the window of the car, saw the tape box on the seat, and said, "Have you been down on Music Row with that tape?"

He talked with a decided lisp. The question, from a total stranger, surprised me.

I swallowed and managed to choke out a "Yes, sir," trying to straighten up in the seat and push my hair back from my eyes at the same time.

Without a word he leaned across me and grabbed hold of the tape box. "Give me that! That's how girls end up on skid row."

Jerry Chesnut owned a vacuum cleaner business—and a gold-colored Cadillac. He was successful and rich. He lived in a beautiful home on the lake in the suburb of Hendersonville. He was also an aspiring songwriter and had come to know Mickey by trading at the service station. Earlier, when he had stopped in, Mickey had been playing my tape. He had paused in the middle of signing his ticket and asked Mickey who that was on the tape. When Mickey told him it was his wife, Jerry said, "She's good. I think she can make it. I might even be able to help her."

Jerry Chesnut had friends at Monument Records in Hendersonville. "They like what they heard," Jerry said excitedly when he called three days later. "But they want to change your name. They have Jeannie Seely, you know, and she just won the award for the most promising female vocalist of the year. They think two Jeannies would be too much. They want to record you, but as Tina Stephens."

"But that's not my name," I stuttered. "Nobody back home would know who Tina Stephens is."

It was almost two weeks later when I heard from Jerry again. "I've got your contract," he said. "They're ready to sign you up. But first they want you to attend the disc jockey convention. They think it'll be good for you to meet the disc jockeys who are coming to town."

"What about my name?" I asked.

"Well, they are still talking about Tina Stephens, but I think they'll drop it if we stay after them."

Jerry lived several miles out in Hendersonville, but I soon found myself driving back and forth to his house to go over the material I was to present to Monument.

I spent a lot of time at Jerry's house. Both he and his wife drove Cadillacs and wore expensive clothes. I was impressed. Mickey was too busy to go with me, so I'd drive out at night and sit in his den, and we'd go over all our plans for the future with Monument.

I liked Jerry. And trusted him. He was obviously a man about town with a number of friends. But he always treated me like a lady. There was something unselfish in his efforts for me, and I was grateful.

The disc jockey convention was held at the old Andrew Jackson Hotel in downtown Nashville. I loved it. I loved being crushed into an elevator with 20 people, all with cocktail glasses in their hands, spilling drinks all over each other, laughing, shouting, so crowded you couldn't breathe. It thrilled me when someone in the elevator looked down at me and said, "Connie Smith ought to sue you for looking so much like her."

I winced when the people from Monument introduced me to all the disc jockeys. "This is the newest voice in Nashville, Tina Stephens. We're getting ready to sign her to a big contract."

Later I met Monument's newest artist, a buxom blonde named Dolly Parton. One of the deejays later pulled me aside and said, "With your deep voice, you're a natural." Then pointing to Dolly, "But that blonde with the squeaky voice'll never make it—not in Nashville." I was dumb enough to believe he knew what he was talking about.

When they drove me home after the convention, I was so excited and hyped up I could hardly wait to see Mickey and tell him all about it. But Mickey was tired. It had been a long day and the traffic into the gas station had been unusually heavy because of a football game at Vanderbilt University.

"They introduced me to all the biggies," I said. "They told everyone that 'Tina Stephens is gonna be the number one singer in Nashville.' "

"I thought you weren't going to let them call you Tina," Mickey said, leaning back on the sofa and reaching for some peanuts, never taking his eyes off the TV set.

I started to answer him, but I realized he wasn't listening. He was beside me but a thousand miles away.

"Okay, so what if I do have to make a few changes. A girl can't have her way all the time. This is a big business and everyone has to compromise. I'll never compromise on the big things. But insisting on being called Jeannie Riley isn't much."

I looked down at Mickey. He had put his head in my lap and was fast asleep. I shook him awake. "I need someone to talk to."

He straightened up, and yawned.

"Then talk," he said.

"But you're not listening."

"I'm doing the best I can. What do you want to say?"

I just sat there, staring at the TV, seeing nothing. Thinking: *Why can't he be exciting like those deejays were today? Why is it all he does is come home from work, drink a beer, eat supper, watch TV and go to sleep?*

"I love you," I said.

I felt him nod his head against my shoulder. "Okay," he said softly, "I know you do."

I wanted to scream. I wanted him to tell me he loved me. Not just once but a thousand times. Why couldn't he take me out to the Andrew Jackson? Why'd he have to wear those dirty uniforms all the time? Why couldn't he look like real people rather than like a gas station cowboy?

But he was asleep. I got up and turned off the TV. He wakened, yawned and said, "I gotta open up in the morning," and headed to bed.

I was too frustrated to cry. I just sat there, thinking, dreaming. It really didn't make any difference. Big things were about to happen.

I had been sitting in Jerry Chesnut's den for almost three hours watching television. I thought it was strange. He had asked me to come out, said he needed to share a few things with me. But all we had done was sit. I was growing edgy, feeling I should be home with Mickey, when he finally spoke up.

"Did Ed Hamilton call you today?"

"No, was he supposed to?"

Something was wrong. The day before at Monument I had run into Ed Hamilton who was one of the executives there. "Well, there's Jeannie Riley," he had said. He had looked at me strangely then left the room. *Why had he called me Jeannie,* I wondered, *since he had been insisting my name was Tina?*

I told Jerry what had happened the day before.

"That son of a ____," Jerry muttered.

"Hey, what's going on?" I asked.

"Ed was supposed to be out here tonight. I guess he just left it to me to break the bad news to you."

"What bad news?" I asked, feeling my mouth go dry.

"It doesn't look like Monument is going to record you after all." Then Jerry went ahead to explain that one of their big artists had blown up when she heard I was to be recorded. When she threatened to leave, they bumped me from their label.

I did a lot of driving around that night, furious at the insecure singer who was afraid I would take her place.

Why did people do things like that to one another? I had thought the music industry was one big happy family, just as they appeared on TV and on the stage of the Grand Ole Opry. I thought there was room for everybody. If Connie Smith could stay number one, and Loretta Lynn could be number one, then why couldn't I join them? There should be room for lots of number ones.

I finally got home and told Mickey. He tried to console me, but he was as empty as I. All we could do was lie there in bed together, me crying and him trying to tell me there were a lot more recording companies than Monument. He finally drifted off to sleep, and I lay there in the darkness thinking, *I'm back to me and my little tape.*

The next day I stayed home, sitting by my little tape player listening to my voice coming off that Wilburn Brothers tape. I played it over and over. Suddenly I was back in Anson, in the little house on stilts, wanting to belong. Needing to be somebody. Then I realized that at that moment, back home, Helen's little girl, Lori, was the Miss Merry Christmas nominee for the Christmas parade. I looked out the window of our apartment, imagining the parade was coming down the street. "Hi, Lori! Hi, Lori!" I cried, waving my hand and jumping up and down.

The tape had run out and the player was humming, going nowhere—the music over. I wasn't in Anson, I was in Nashville. I began to cry. I really hadn't seen Lori go by in the red convertible with the other little girls. She wasn't here, she was there. I picked up Kim, hugged her and turned off the machine. It was all make believe. Maybe my dream was make believe. There wasn't any star to hitch my wagon to, just a burned-out bulb in the closet and a little tape on a little tape player.

The next day I was back on the streets. I called Capitol Records and by dropping Jerry Chesnut's name I was able to make an appointment for that afternoon. The young boy who was in charge of "A & R" (artists and repertoire) told me he was the one appointed to work with new people. He listened to the tape.

"Not bad," he said, as he rewound it. "There's some good singing here. The one you're really good on is 'Don't Let Me Keep You If You Don't Want to Stay.' Do you have any others?"

I felt my heart sink. That was all I had. He told me he'd like to hear some more of my own songs and then said to go home and write some more.

"Bring them back, and I'll give you a listen," he said. "Right now we're full up, but we'll take your name and when we have an opening we'll give you a call. You're good, but you just don't have enough stuff. We've got to have something pretty special to send to our board in Los Angeles for approval."

That was all new to me. "You mean you have to have approval of a committee before you can sign up a new artist?" I asked.

"That's the way it is," he said. "At least, that's the way it is if you go with the big boys."

The fellow took my number and said he would get in touch with me.

But he never did.

Jerry Chesnut, through his advertising connections with a Nashville radio station, had met a disc jockey named Pete Terry. He said Pete might be able to help me since he was a friend of Phil Blackman who managed Black Rose Records out of New York. Black Rose had just signed the most promising male singer in Nashville and was looking for a fresh female voice.

"Maybe you shouldn't hold out for the big labels," Jerry said. Monument wasn't big enough to suit me, but I had compromised with them, just as I had compromised on my name. Now along comes Black Rose which was even smaller. What other standards would I be required to drop before I finally made it?

Jerry drove me out to the radio station and introduced me to Pete Terry who listened to my tape. He was a little cocky, but he seemed to know his business. And he promised to introduce me to Phil Blackman.

I looked up at Pete. Six feet tall and husky. Dark hair with a slightly receding hairline. The collar of his shirt was casually open, and his tie hung loose. He grinned and went into the studio to make a copy of the tape to send to Blackman in New York.

Several days later, Pete Terry called me.

"I have a letter from Blackman," he said excitedly. "He likes you. He said he thought you had as much potential as Connie Smith and wants to get with you right after the first of the year and do a recording."

"How sure is that?" I asked, my heart beating in my throat.

"You can trust Phil Blackman," Pete said. "If he says it, he means it. He'll not let you down."

I didn't know it at the time, but Pete Terry had just told me the biggest lie I had ever heard.

6

The Black Rose

It was early February when I walked into Black Rose Records. The offices were in an old funeral home which, in looking back on it, seems strangely symbolic. The front office was painted dark red and only the record logo, a green vine with two black rose clusters, gave color to the otherwise drab room. I came alone without Mickey or Kim because I had heard through gossip that Connie Smith had divorced her husband Jerry because he had insisted on being with her so much during her recording sessions and appearances. People said that Jerry didn't fit into the Nashville scene, that he interfered with her career. Since I didn't want anything to spoil my career, it seemed best to leave Kim at home with a baby sitter and Mickey at the service station. If I was to make it I would have to make it alone.

I expected to find a cigar-smoking, pot-bellied New York executive sitting behind the desk. Instead, I walked in and there sat God's gift to all women. I couldn't tell how old Phil Blackman was—30, 40—it didn't make any difference. Dark, wavy hair, greased down in the style of the time, pulled to a ducktail in the back. His collar was turned up in Elvis Presley style. He stood, walked around the desk to greet me, and I suddenly felt a strange shakiness in my knees. That this was the man who was going to make me a star seemed too good to be true.

I brought the contract home and showed it to Mickey. He wanted to know all about Phil Blackman, but I was suddenly hesitant to describe him.

All I could remember were Blackman's words: "The girl can sing, and she's beautiful, too." I was noticed. I counted. Someone really worthwhile was paying attention to me.

That night I began fantasizing about Phil Blackman. Maybe he was falling in love with me. It was a dumb thing for me to do. I didn't know anything about him. If only Mickey would tell me I was beautiful.

That night, as usual, Mickey went to sleep on the sofa with his head in my lap. I kept waking him to say, "I love you," over and over. It was as if I did not say it, something evil and sinister could take over my life. Finally he said, "Honey, I appreciate you telling me this, but I know it without you having to say it every few minutes."

This deeply annoyed me. "The day will come when you'll give anything to hear me say I love you."

He sat up and looked at me. "Now, what does that mean?"

I was shocked, but I wasn't going to back down. "I don't know," I said. "All I know is, I need you, and you're always too tired to even listen."

I spent every day for the next week at Black Rose Records. Phil was going to be in town for only a short while, and I needed to get everything done while he was there. I found a baby sitter, which released me to ramble—and dream—with Phil.

Phil had an apartment out on Murfreesboro Road near the airport. It seemed natural that I would begin meeting him when he came in from New York to discuss business and listen to tapes. I believed every word he told me. I believed him when he said my star was going to shine brighter than any star in Nashville. Why not? I had always believed this.

"You know," he whispered one day at the office while I was sitting at a desk working on a song revision, "I think I'm in love with you."

"You're what?"

He grinned, leaned down and kissed me on my cheek. "You're so pure. So innocent. Don't you know when I'm just talking?"

"You mean you're not in love with me?" I asked simply.

He threw back his head and laughed. "I mean I am in love with you, but I'm willing to wait until you can say it back."

It was heady stuff for a small town girl from Texas. How could I share something like this with Mickey?

One day, out at his apartment where we were drinking coffee and listening to tapes, he reached over the table, took my hand and said, "One of these days you will look up at me from a pillow and tell me you love me."

I giggled and pulled my hand away. "You shouldn't say things like that. I might believe you."

But I did believe him. And I wanted him to say it again. I was tired of Mickey going to sleep with the chickens. I was tired of dirty service station uniforms and brogans with grease on the soles. I was tired of cooking meals and watching them get cold because Mickey was late. His 12-hour days often ran to 14 hours. I was already tired of the routine. *Surely,* I thought, *Mickey is getting fed up too.* It never occurred to me how subtly I was letting down the bars. But what started with a thrill had turned into a fantasy and was now developing into full-fledged desire.

Phil returned to New York for several weeks but called me as soon as he arrived back in Nashville. Could I meet him? He said we needed to practice some songs.

I phoned for a baby sitter and eagerly drove to Phil's apartment. We sat on the couch. Talking at first. He seemed extra-sensitive to my emotional needs that night. Soon he was kissing me, and before long I had followed him upstairs. Mickey and Kim suddenly belonged to another world.

"You know that I'd like to see you all the time," he whispered. "If I could ever quit being so busy. More than anything else I want to be with you."

He took me on an imaginary trip in a sailboat, describing the wind rippling the water, the little waves splashing against the rocks, the feel of the spray against our faces. He was sensitive, so sensitive. He talked his way so smoothly and expertly into the privacy of my life that when I broke my marriage vows I hardly even realized I had broken them. It seemed so right. Without even looking back I slipped the rope from the unpainted dock and let the wind catch my sails. I was off, flying over the water free from every inhibition or guilt or memory. Just Phil and me—flying toward our destiny.

He wore a certain cologne. Every letter I received from him, whether it was a memo in his office or a letter from New York, carried that certain smell. I hid the notes under the mattress, then in my closet.

"I don't know what we're going to do with this wonderful thing that's happened to us."

"How could any two people in history feel the way we do?"

I began to learn little things about him, things that made me love him even more. He had been orphaned as a child. He had to work long hours. It aroused all the natural mother instincts in me.

Poor Mickey, I kept thinking, *all he does is work, drink beer and sleep.* If he only knew me. If he only knew what was going on in my heart. It was sad, knowing that I was drifting from him. But the boat was in motion, and I could not remain on the dock any longer.

Once the seal was broken, it was an easy thing to fall into a routine. First there had been the thrill, then a fantasy, then a desire, now it was a habit. When it really dawned on me what I was doing, there seemed no way to change it. When I drove home at night the guilt and fear consumed me. Where could it lead but to some kind of disaster? Yet I continued to fantasize about our life together.

To compensate for my guilt feelings, I began to withdraw from Mickey. It was as though I could justify my relationship with Phil by being faithful to him—and pulling away from Mickey. Adultery, I concluded, was the same thing as unfaithfulness: as long as I was not unfaithful to Phil, I could justify what I was doing. I would stay up long hours at night until Mickey had gone to sleep. I neglected him as much as possible. It was easy since he asked so little of me. As long as there was only one man in my life, I could live with myself.

Though deep in deception, something in me had been set free. Living on an emotional high, I sang better, felt better and dreamed of higher things than ever before. It was as if Phil had taken me to a high mountain and shown me all the kingdoms of the world and said, "All this power will I give you. If you will love me, it is all yours."

And I had suddenly possessed all the earth.

When I asked Phil why he didn't call me when he was in New York for long periods of time, he said it was out of consideration for my family. He didn't want to put me under pressure. He had a deep concern for Mickey, he said, and felt that his calling might cause problems. I was touched by his seeming tenderness and consideration.

During the months that followed Phil released one single I had done—a 45 rpm record. It was a shoddy piece of work. Even I knew that. I began to wonder if I had made a mistake. Had I settled for too little? He wasn't promoting me. He wasn't pushing my music or my career. He kept telling me I had potential, and one day I would be known all over the world. He was, he said, my key to the door of success. But so far there had been only one pathetic release.

Then it dawned slowly upon me that our time together was not really an expression of love. It was only physical. I was torn with inner conflicts. Feelings of love for him. Feelings of hate toward myself. The realization came that the physical act of love was not love at all. My heart really yearned for something else, something much deeper. And always, after it was over, there were the periods of sadness. The guilt was overwhelming.

I had allowed Phil to invade the areas of my life that should have been reserved for Mickey. But neither man had been able to touch the areas of my deepest need. The center of my being still cried out for real love.

It all surfaced one night in his apartment. We had been on the sofa together. Phil had gotten up to go to the bathroom. The guilt of all the past evenings in that house—on that sofa—seemed to descend on me during those moments. I turned my face toward the cushions and stopped trying to hold back the tears. Why did it always have to wind up like this? Where would it all end?

Suddenly the room was filled with a flashing light and a weird, unearthly laughter. Startled, I looked up. Phil was standing in the middle of the room, taking flash pictures of me. "Great pose!" he laughed, and the flashing went off again. I was momentarily blinded as the strobe flash reflected off my tears. I screamed, reaching for my clothing on the floor.

"That ought to make a great record jacket picture," he laughed.

I came off the sofa fighting, yelling and screaming.

"Hey, calm down," he said, dancing back. "It's only a flash attachment. I was just trying to scare you."

Stunned, my heart beating wildly, I sat back down on the couch. "You mean you weren't taking pictures?" I asked.

"I wouldn't do a thing like that to you, would I?" he joshed. "I was just playing around with this little electronic flash. See?" He held it out, but my eyes were still dilated from the bright flash, and I could hardly see. I took his word for it and sank back on the sofa pillows.

"Do you really love me?" I pleaded. "I mean, this is more than just physical, isn't it?"

"You're just a little girl," he said tenderly. "You don't even understand what love is all about."

"Love is having someone who really cares about you," I said simply. "Love is kindness. It's having someone who won't take advantage of you. It lets you tell the truth, the total truth, to each other and only wants the very best for the other person. It lasts forever and nothing can destroy it."

"That sounds like something you learned in Sunday school back in Texas," he laughed, reaching for a cigarette.

"But I love you," I argued. "Why else would I be here like this? I'm not hiding anything from you. You know all about me."

"That's because there isn't much to know," he said coldly. "But you don't know all about me. You don't know anything about me."

I felt a chill enter the room, a dark chill. I shuddered

and balled up tighter on the couch.

"That's not so," I said, my voice quivering a little. "You said you loved me, and I believed you. And I love you. That's why I'm here with you."

"You don't love me," he half sneered, blowing smoke across the room. "You're not here because you love me. You're here because you want something from me. You want me to release your record. You want me to make you a star. That's what you want from me. What I want from you is something different."

I was having difficulty breathing. "Please, Phil, please don't say these things. We're gonna get married. We're gonna be together all our lives . . ."

I got up from the sofa and started toward him.

"Sit down!" he shouted. "You're just a stupid little girl. I don't love you. Don't you know that? We've just been playing games. The same games everyone plays. Sure, you're a beautiful girl, and I'm attracted to you. But I've got a wife and two boys; I have my own life to live. There's not room for you, too."

I was crying. How could this happen to me? I had seen it in the movies, but that was not real. This was real. I felt used, abused, lost, alone. I wanted to throw up. Why hadn't he told me about his wife and children? But then I had never asked him. It never occurred to me he might be married, despite the fact I was. How could I be so naive?

My voice was very small. "Where does your family live?"

"New York," he said, grinding out his cigarette. "Did you think I had been waiting just for you all my life? This is my second marriage. Everything was fine with you until you tried to get serious. But you don't know how to play the game. You want to get involved."

"But that's what love is," I said, trying to hold back the tears. "Love is wanting to be together. Living together. Sharing your life with each other."

"That's more Sunday school talk," he said coldly. "There ain't no love in this world, baby. It's all hard knocks. You take what you get and to hell with everyone else."

"But you said we were meant for each other. You've said that yourself. You said there was no one else in this world but me. You said you wanted to be with me the rest of your life."

"Talk is cheap, little girl. And it's all part of the game we human animals play to get what we want. I can tell you a girl right now who has had four number one records, and believe me, it wasn't her singing that got her there."

I left his apartment utterly horrified. Embarrassed. Ashamed. I felt as if I had been used, like a paper napkin to wipe someone's greasy mouth, and then thrown into the gutter. Worthless. Memories returned of the sadness I felt in childhood sitting in the Baptist Sunday school listening to the story of Genesis. I remember wanting to cry when God, big and mean, told Adam and Eve they had to leave their beautiful garden. They had lived there all their lives. They had even named all the animals. Then God came along and drove them out and put that bright shining angel at the gate with a huge sword. I could picture the angel, standing at the gate of the garden, frightening away poor Adam and Eve who, bent and weeping, went away into darkness.

I thought of Kim, back at the house, sleeping innocently in her little bed. Would she be driven out of the garden, too, because of me?

I drove slowly into the city—unwilling to go straight home. In front of me loomed the huge white pillars of Nashville's Parthenon. It was the exact replica of the Grecian temple dedicated to the virgin goddess Athena. I remembered something: not only did she stand for wisdom and the arts, but for moral purity. The flood lights reflected off the green grass and shimmering white stone. I wondered if the spirit of the virgin would haunt me, if I was cursed forever.

I wanted to blame Phil, but I was as guilty as he. If only there were just evil and good people, I thought. If it were that way, it would be easy to separate the evil from the rest of us and destroy it. But the line between good and evil cuts through every human heart. And who is willing to destroy a piece of himself?

7

Harper Valley PTA

One of the stipulations in my contract with Black Rose Records was that Pete Terry would be my manager. I liked that. Having this tall, handsome deejay with his shy smile to help me made me feel comfortable. Secure. Pete lined up for me a few singing engagements for which he received a percentage.

Six months after the showdown with Phil Blackman I went to Las Vegas for my first appearance there as the opening act for Johnny Paycheck at the Golden Nugget. It was early fall 1967, and Phil happened to be there too. He did everything he could to get my attention with little things. Winks. Touches on the shoulder. Small things. I still cared deeply for him, but the idea of being with him was now repulsive.

He came to my room one night. I was reluctant to let him in and kept him standing at the door.

"What bugs you?" he said, annoyed. "You've got your name on the marquee. That's what you wanted all along. Now it's time for me to collect. Don't you push at me like that."

"You're not gonna bully me—never again," I said firmly. "I've learned a few things, too."

"You seem to forget who pulls the strings in this business," he said pointedly. But I was as stubborn as he was pushy. He finally left in a rage.

I called Mickey that night. I told him I wanted to come home. I was fed up. Singing to a bunch of drunks in a night club was a downer. I could have added that each time I reached for my star, I got a handful of slime instead. If the only way a girl could make it to the top was to sell her soul to the man who had the power to get her there, then it wasn't worth it.

Later, when I wrote "A Country Girl's Lament," I summed it all up:

> I won't muddy my stream of inspiration for a meal,
> I won't cast my pearls before swine,
> I'd rather starve to death, than later regret
> That I'd sold my soul for a dime.*
>> A Country Girl's Lament
>> Jeannie C. Riley

I began longing for Mickey as I had known him back in Anson. Kim was now two years old, but I was unable to give her my best. I didn't sleep much that night, wanting to go home—but not knowing where home really was.

I had never drunk hard liquor before. But in Las Vegas I discovered such things as Singapore Slings, Screwdrivers and drinks where the alcohol was hidden. You could pour it down, get drunk and never have to taste the alcohol.

I was miserable—and my singing was worse. I lost my desire, and by the time the week was over, I didn't care whether I ever sang again or not. There was something heavy about the city, as though a smothering spirit was hanging over the strip.

The last night in Las Vegas, when I knew Phil Blackman was headed back to Nashville, I returned to my hotel room after the show. Alone in the early morning darkness, I wrote Phil a 30-page letter. I begged him to release me from whatever spell he had over me. I described the multiple feelings he aroused in me: love, hate, physical desire, guilt. I begged him to free me from my contract with Black Rose Records.

I did not mail the letter. I was afraid to mail it. Sometimes it's easier to remain in bondage than to admit you've made a mistake.

It was late January before I finally mustered the courage to contact Phil again. I called him at his office in Nashville and told him I had a letter I wanted him to read. He asked if I was trying to get a release from Black Rose. I said yes, but I wanted him to read the letter first. He said he would be willing to talk about a release but only if I came to talk with him in person. I was desperate. I agreed to come by the office and talk to him.

It had snowed that morning, and the driving was tricky. I managed to get to his office but refused to take off my coat or boots. I just sat there on the front edge of the chair, the big letter in my hand, and asked if he would read it.

"We can't read it here," he said. I did not know it at the time, but his wife had moved to Nashville, and he was afraid she might get wind of what had been going on between us. "Let's go somewhere, and I'll read what you've written."

We got in his car and drove. I didn't know where he was taking me, but I was like a robot. I knew this was my chance to break things off. We ended up at his secretary's apartment. I thought it was odd that he had a key and seemed to know his way around, but that was incidental to our real reason for being there. He took my coat and then the letter. I stood to one side, looking out the window at the snowflakes falling gently on the dirty streets below, covering all the filth with a blanket of whiteness. He read the letter slowly. I hoped the words from my heart would touch his, too.

"Okay," he said as he finished. "I'll give you your release." Then he turned on the old charm again. "You know I still love you," he said gently, coming to where I was standing at the window and slipping his arms around me from behind. "I'm sorry for all the harsh things I've said. Maybe I've been too honest with you, but everything I've told you has been true. Sure, I've gotten angry, but it was never with you. It's just that I knew you had all the makings of a great star—and still do. I just wanted to be there when your star flashed to life. I wanted to feel I had a small part in making it happen."

I didn't believe him. Not anymore. But I was afraid to argue. I knew he would not give me the release until I went with him, one more time, back into the nightmare of the past. It was 3 p.m. when I returned to the window and stood staring at the gentle snow, still falling, and wondered deep within if anything could cover the stain of my guilt. Could I ever be clean again? I was ashamed. Humiliated. Yet I knew I had finally put that chapter behind me. He handed me the release. I'd paid a high price for my freedom.

I got home that night and wanted to tell Mickey what had happened. God knows how badly I needed to talk to him about it. But I could not. How could I tell him a thing was all over when he didn't know it had ever started?

Three important things happened to me that spring. When I had been in Las Vegas opening for Johnny Paycheck, his producer, Aubrey Mayhew, had heard me sing. He was the first producer to actually seek me out. He wanted to know if I would be willing to cut a demo tape for his company, Little Darlin' Records.

Although Mayhew reminded me of Phil, with his Elvis Presley ducktail haircut and suave mannerisms, I immediately liked him. He had been producing Paycheck and seemed to be doing a good job. Pete thought it would be good for me to let him cut a single—45 rpm—just to see how it would go. After all, to come along on the same label of a big male star like Paycheck couldn't hurt my career.

Mayhew told me I had an "infectious" voice and said he was certain he could turn me into a big star. It was a line, I later discovered, used by all slick producers who tried to sign up newcomers to Nashville. Maybe he really believed it; more likely he said it to get me under contract just in case anything did develop. It made no difference. I believed it because I desperately wanted to believe something good could happen to me.

Signing a contract, I later discovered, is a big thing. Most young singers are so eager to get "under contract" they forget what it all might mean in the future. That's the reason most producers try to "tie a singer up" not just for that one record but for all her future records as well—just in case the singer makes it big later on.

After signing a contract with Mayhew, I cut a single record for him which never amounted to anything and some demos that were later released in an album. The arrangement with Mayhew's record company never really went anywhere; in fact, we wound up in contract difficulties. But cutting that single and releasing the album did bring me temporary encouragement.

A second important event that spring was meeting a woman who was to become one of my closest and most trusted friends. Her name was Jerri Clark.

Jerri's husband, Royce, was a song writer and friend of a producer named Shelby Singleton, who was to bcome a key figure in my life. Royce spent time hanging around Mickey's service station, and it was there I met Jerri, and immediately I fell in love with her as a kind of mama.

Close to six feet tall and big around as well, Jerri towered over me. Sensing my need for a shoulder to cry on, she opened herself to be my confidante as well. She rolled my hair. She looked after little Kim. She had let me cry on her shoulder, confessing all the things I needed to confess to Mickey but couldn't.

Kim, who was just beginning to talk well, called her "Kinda-Mama." The name stuck, for she was my Kinda-Mama as well.

The third important thing to happen that spring was an offer from Jerry Chesnut to go to work for him. Jerry had decided to leave the vacuum cleaner business and concentrate on his music.

Jerry knew how much I wanted to be near the music business, and since this young company could not afford an expensive secretary, he offered me the job working in his office at Passkey Music on Music Row. I took it eagerly, and my education about music companies advanced rapidly. I discovered that girls were constantly coming in off the street with or without their demos or were calling, wanting help. Jerry was a big brother in so many ways, and I loved and respected him for it. But my fears were working over-time. I was still hurting from the Phil Blackman affair, and

I suspected all producers and studio bosses might be the same way.

Occasionally Jerry received a phone call about some Nashville gossip. After he had finished talking, he would come out of his office, sit on the edge of my desk and spiel it off.

I would interrupt, almost crying. "Please, Jerry. Don't tell me that . . ."

"Come on now," he would joke. "Since you never get around very much and don't know what's going on in Nashville, I just thought you'd like to know what goes on after hours."

I wanted to cry. But I couldn't tell him anything. I couldn't tell anyone. Not Mickey. Not Jerry. Not even Kinda-Mama. Yet all the time it was like a big balloon inside me, getting bigger and bigger. I felt if I didn't tell someone about what had happened between Phil and me, I would explode.

Finally one day I did explode. It was a slow afternoon in early May. A friend of Jerry's had stopped by Passkey, and Jerry had pulled a bottle of gin out of his drawer. The two men were sitting in the outer office near my desk, pouring each other drinks.

"What about me?" I blurted out.

Jerry grinned and shook his head.

My early training in the Baptist church and the influence of Grandpa Moore had given me a strong aversion to liquor. Aside from that one time in Las Vegas, I had stayed away from it. Maybe it went back to Mama's reaction to any drinking Daddy did. Mama was pretty docile most of the time, but when it came to alcohol, she didn't like it in the house and said so. So daddy drank his beer in the little shed behind the house. Mama knew what was going on and tolerated it. Only when she was eyeball to eyeball with it was she liable to explode. And when that happened, it was mighty to behold.

But Mama wasn't there that afternoon in Jerry's office. And it wasn't beer—it was gin. While the men were sipping their drinks and talking together, they didn't notice that I kept filling my glass. It didn't take much. I had to go to the bathroom several times and the last time I emerged, I couldn't walk straight. Suddenly, without warning, I decided to shout. It was a loud, echoing shout, and when I heard the noise, I decided to run. Down the hall I sped, lickety-split, through the door of the office and landed on top of the desk like a cowboy jumping his horse. Whirling around, I let out a Tarzan whoop and landed back on the floor— flat on my back.

"Oh, no!" Jerry shouted, leaping to his feet and almost overturning his chair.

His friend, who had stepped in the outer office, ran back. Immediately Jerry locked the outer door. "Don't let anyone in," he said, alarmed. "This could ruin you," he said, trying to get me to sit down.

But I didn't care. For the first time in months I felt free. I felt like singing. I felt like dancing. And I did. All at the same time.

Jerry frantically phoned a local food joint. "Send up some black coffee at once."

For almost an hour he poured coffee down me. "I can't send you home like this," he said. "Mickey would skin us both."

By that time I had calmed down, stopped my laughing and giggling and was nauseated. The first time they got me to the bathroom. The second time I used the trash basket in Jerry's office.

"Let's get out of here," Jerry said. "I'll ride you around in the car until your head clears. Then you go home and go to bed."

He told his friend good-by, locked the office and put me in his car. We had no sooner left the parking lot than I began to cry.

"What's really wrong?" he asked tenderly.

It was all I needed. For the next hour, as he drove down the quiet tree-shaded streets of suburban Nashville, I told him about Phil Blackman.

Royce Clark, Kinda-Mama's husband, was spending a lot of time with Mickey at the service station. Like most singers and composers in Nashville, he believed he would one day strike it rich in the music field. Not only that, he believed

I was just the girl to make his songs come to life.

He had written a number of songs that he wanted Shelby Singleton, the producer at Plantation Records, to hear. One of them in particular he felt was "just right" for my voice. It was called "The Old Town Drunk" and was the typical sarcastic ballad of the old drunk that everyone in town made fun of until one day they found his hat floating in the river and his shoes next to the river bank. The whole town got concerned and started dragging the river looking for his body. All the while the old town drunk was up on the side of the hill, overlooking the entire scene, laughing. He finally came down and told the folks he was glad he was so well thought of.

It was just the kind of cutesie song you could sing and get saucy and sarcastic since the lyrics reflected the mood of the nation. The Vietnam war, with all its hypocrisy, had stirred the anger of the youth of America. People were confused. The nation was frustrated. To express dissent against the war indicated you were unpatriotic. And if Nashville believed in one thing, it was patriotism. So one way to express the frustration of a generation who felt the war was morally wrong, but was caught in it at the same time, was to publish sarcastic songs about another kind of hypocrisy. Even though "The Old Town Drunk" was really a man's song—the kind Johnny Paycheck could have made a killing on—Royce wanted me to record it so he could give it to Shelby Singleton.

Well, "The Old Town Drunk" never made it. But it was the vehicle which got my voice to Shelby Singleton. When Pete Terry played it for him one day he asked, "Who's that girl doing the singing?"

"Her name's Jeannie Riley," Pete said. Then he added, "I've got another tape out in the car if you'd like to hear some more."

Singleton listened to the Wilburn Brothers tape. Leaning back in his chair he smiled slightly. "You get me that girl," he said. "Tom Hall has just written a song, and if I match his song with her voice, we'll cut us a million-seller."

Pete was at my house in less than an hour. "Listen, Jeannie," he almost panted, "this is it. If anybody can put you over, it's Shelby Singleton."

I knew a little about Singleton. He had been a producer with Mercury before he branched out on his own label. He wasn't a big time producer, but he had a fine track record. In fact, shortly before, he had cut *three* one-million sellers in one day: "Ahab the Arab" with Ray Stevens, "One of Us" with Patti Page and "Walk On By" with Leroy VanDyke. He knew the business.

"What's the song?" I asked.

Pete tried to explain. "A tunesmith named Tom Hall has written this song about the hypocrisy that goes on in a small town. It centers around some stuffy people in the Parent-Teachers Association and how they judge other parents until one mom takes them on, comes to the meeting and names all their sins in public. It's called 'Harper Valley PTA.' Another girl cut a demo tape on it but Shelby didn't like her voice."

"Get me the tape," I said. "I want to hear the song before I give you an answer."

"What's wrong with you?" Pete said. "Here's your chance to hit it big—the chance for all of us to hit it big—and you want to play around."

I was stubborn. "Let me hear the tape, and then I'll give you an answer."

Pete was back early the next morning with a demo tape. I didn't like it. The other song on the demo tape was "The Ballad of Louise." It was the story of a woman who found her husband with her best friend, Louise, and she then shot Louise. I told Jerry that I liked "The Ballad of Louise" better than "Harper Valley PTA."

"I wonder why?" Jerry quipped.

"I don't want to do 'Harper Valley PTA,'" I shot back. "There's something about it I don't like."

That afternoon Pete Terry, Royce Clark and Kinda-Mama all ganged up on me. "Jeannie, you're a fool," Pete said. "Shelby Singleton may not be a major label, but when he gets excited about something, he can make it move."

I finally agreed to take off that afternoon and go over and talk to Shelby at Plantation Records on Belmont Boulevard. I had a strange feeling when I walked into his office. There was something ominous about Singleton—a chunky man with bushy black hair—that I didn't like. But Pete kept urging me on, saying it was just right for me.

Singleton said flatly, "We'll cut a pop hit on this."

I blurted out, "Oh, no. I'm a country singer. I don't want to be a pop singer."

Shelby thought that was funny. But he continued, "Of course we'll have to change your name. There're too many Jeannies in Nashville already."

Well, I agreed with that. There was Jeannie Seely, Jeannie Shepard, Jeannie Pruett, Jeannie O'Neal, Jeannie Steakley . . . Shelby wanted to call me Rhonda Renae.

"I don't like it," I said softly. Afraid to speak out, yet knowing if I didn't, no one else would. "Couldn't we at least use Rhonda Jean Riley?"

"That's no good," Singleton said. He reached for a brown cigarette—specially made with his initials on it. "We need a name that will be unique. When you say 'Loretta' everybody knows you're talking about Loretta Lynn. The same is true with Tammy Wynette. We need a name that everyone will know, without having to make explanation. There are no Rhondas in Nashville. Rhonda Riley ain't a good stage name. We'll stick with Rhonda Renae."

I looked at Pete. Somehow I wished Mickey were there. But I couldn't picture him sitting there in the office of Plantation Records, his straw cowboy hat pushed back on his head, with his faded jeans and Texas drawl. Pete, as my manager, would have to handle it for me.

"I don't want to sound ugly, Jeannie," Pete said, sensing my hestitation, "but I don't see how I can continue to represent you if you don't sign this contract. People have listened to your tape and turned you down. They say Nashville is full of imitators. Everybody wants to sound like Loretta or Connie or Tammy. Now here's your chance to be different. To set your own course. To let your dream come true. If you turn it down, I don't know where else to go. You'll just have to find another manager."

"But I won't be Jeannie Riley," I said stubbornly. "I'll be Rhonda Renae, whoever she is."

I went ahead and signed the contract. Terrified over what

I had done, I cried all the way home. When Mickey came in from work, he found me at the kitchen table, my face swollen and red, feeling I had just made the biggest mistake of my life.

"What's the matter with you?" Mickey asked, taking one look at my face.

"They talked me into signing the contract," I said. "I think I just signed away another year of my life—maybe more."

"Well, why did you give in? All you have to do is wait until the right offer comes along. We're eating all right, ain't we?"

"That's not it," I replied, still choking out the words. "They said this might be my last chance. They said this could be the biggest thing to come out of Nashville. If I turned it down, I'd be finished."

"Well, no one is gonna put the strong arm on my wife," Mickey said angrily. He picked up the phone and called Pete Terry at his house.

"I ain't gonna tell you but once," Mickey said, his words clipped. "Jeannie's come home crying about that contract she signed. I'll not have it. I want you to tear up that contract. I ain't gonna have her sucked into anything she don't want to do."

Down went the phone.

I looked at Mickey for a long time. He was the only man in the world who I knew would stand up for me in every situation. He was the only man in the world, aside from my daddy, who didn't want to use me. All he wanted was my good. He was my best fan. He played my tape at the service station and talked to his customers about me. He had introduced me to some key people who had tried to help me.

Yet I had let him down in so many ways—and he didn't even know it, didn't even suspect it. He didn't question or accuse when I was frigid in bed. He didn't complain when I took the car and kept it all day, burning up gas. All that mattered to him was my happiness. Phil Blackman had said there was no love in the world, that we're all just a pack of animals—all of whom wanted their own way. Yet here was Mickey Riley, who loved me more than he loved himself.

Pete Terry didn't tear up the contract. The next day he and the others put pressure on me to go ahead with the recording. "I talked with Shelby this afternoon, and he said you could use your own name," Terry assured me. "He also said he would tear up the contract if things didn't go well for you. All he really wants is this one record, and if the record doesn't do anything or you're not happy with it, then he will let you out and not tie you up for an entire year. You can even try to get on RCA if you want."

As usual I gave in—although I was filled with resentment toward them and angry at myself for not having enough guts to say no. And so I promised to come in after work Friday night and cut "Harper Valley PTA" for Shelby Singleton and Plantation Records.

8

Slaying the Music Dragon

On Friday I was angry all day. I felt all my friends had betrayed me. I didn't believe Pete when he said Shelby Singleton would tear up my contract. I didn't believe they'd let me use my own name. I didn't believe any of them were doing it for my benefit. I was mad at Pete for saying he would quit if I didn't take the offer. I was mad at the whole world.

I closed the office at 5 o'clock and walked next door to Columbia Studio. It was a hot, humid evening. I was dressed in black toreador pants. My orange and black blouse was sticking to my back. I didn't care; I just wanted to get it over with.

Shelby kept saying the song was "just right" for my voice. Just right to catch the angry mood of a nation fed up with hypocrisy. I glanced at the music and listened as Jerry Kennedy, the session leader, began his cadence countdown. I began to tap my foot to the beat, my black square-toed shoes going "click, click" on the floor of the studio. I stepped up to the mike. The guitars began strummin', Jerry's dobro was going "dwoang, dwoang," and suddenly I was into the song.

From the very first word my mood and the lyrics came together in a magical blend.

> I want to tell you all a story about a Harper Valley
> widowed wife
> Who had a teenage daughter who attended Harper
> Valley Junior High . . .

I stood close to the mike and let it pour out, sassing everything I hated. There wasn't a sound as the last echo of the guitars faded. Then I heard one of the musicians say, "Great Gawd A'mighty."

It had taken 15 minutes to cut the first tape. Shelby's short, blonde, wife was in the studio and listened to me sing it the first time. She had heard the James Brown and Joe Tex phrase, "Sock it to me, baby." No one ever used terms like that in country music, but she suggested the change.

"Why don't you all change that last line to 'the day my mama socked it to the Harper Valley PTA'?"

Everybody in the studio said, "Yeah. Right on! Let's cut it again."

So I went back in the studio and did one more take. Suddenly I was in it. The lyrics, the music, literally made mc the Harper Valley PTA girl. Caught up in it, I snorted and sneered the anger of the world—my anger at the world. That was it. What the world heard was what was done the second time around in the studio—the dobro licks and all.

The slide dobro was associated with bluegrass music. But Jerry Kennedy, instead of sliding the dobro, picked it with a twangy lick, a sort of "dwoang, dwoang, dwoang" sound. It was just the right sound to match my anger and the saucy, get-even mood of the song.

> I want to tell you all a story about a Harper Valley
> widowed wife
> Who had a teenage daughter who attended Harper
> Valley Junior High.
> Well, her daughter came home one afternoon and didn't
> even stop to play,
> And she said, "Mama, I got a note here from the
> Harper Valley PTA."
> Well, the note said, "Mrs. Johnson, you're wearing your

dresses way too high.
It's reported you've been drinkin' and runnin' around
with men and going wild.
And we don't believe you ought to be bringing up your
little girl this way."
It was signed by the secretary, Harper Valley PTA.
Well, it happened that the PTA was gonna meet that
very afternoon
And they were sure surprised when Mrs. Johnson wore
her miniskirt into the room.
And as she walked up to the blackboard I can still
recall the words she had to say.
She said, "I'd like to address this meeting of the Harper
Valley PTA.
Well, there's Bobby Taylor sitting there. Seven times
he's asked me for a date.
Mrs. Taylor sure seems to use a lot of ice whenever
he's away.
And Mr. Baker, can you tell us why your secretary had
to leave this town,
And shouldn't Widow Jones be told to keep her win-
dow shades all pulled completely down?
Well, Mr. Harper couldn't be here 'cause he stayed too
long at Kelly's Bar again,
And if you'd smell Shirley Thompson's breath, you'd
find she's had a little nip of gin.
And then you have the nerve to tell me you think that
as a mother I'm not fit.
Well, this is just a little Peyton Place, and you're all
Harper Valley hypocrites."
No, I wouldn't put you on, because it really did, it
happened just this way,
The day my mama socked it to the Harper Valley PTA.

>   Words and music by
>   Tom T. Hall

"Harper Valley PTA" was a fascinating blend of explosive
parts. The nation was angry. I was angry. Not at the same
things, for I really didn't care that much about the national
situation nor about small town hypocrisy. I was just angry

at the people around me. Angry at myself for being the kind of woman I was, pushed around by everyone. Angry at being lied to. Angry for believing the lies. And I was ready to sock it to the entire world, which is what I did that last Friday night in July 1968.

The magic continued into the night. I came back after taking a break and recorded "The Ballad of Louise." There was something in my voice that night, and belting out those songs did something for me. Somehow I was able, with my voice, to slay the music dragons of Nashville. Mr. Harper, Bobby Taylor, the Widow Jones and all the other citizens of Harper Valley were my victims. And when it come to recording "Louise," it was Phil Blackman on the point of my lance.

> I had a love, he was mine,
> Said he'd love me all the time,
> I was sure our love was pure,
> If love can be.
> Then one morning, without warning,
> Truth came calling on me . . .
> The hour was late, the night was warm,
> I had the bundle beneath my arm.
> The thought of what I'd soon be doing made me freeze.
> But without fear I found them there just how and
> where I knew they'd be,
> Sleeping; cradled in his arms was Louise.
> Now they've closed those heavy doors,
> I'll never leave here any more,
> But I dare not beg forgiveness on my knees.
> For it was done with careful plans,
> She'll never steal another man,
> For tomorrow they'll bury Louise.*

When I finished, the musicians didn't want to leave. They kept staying on. Everybody kept going back to listen to "Harper Valley PTA" over and over. There was a spell on the song itself.

---

*Ballad of Louise, Naomi Martin © 1968, Shelby Singleton Music, Inc.

Even though it was a closed session, people kept appearing. Somehow the entire building filled with people. One person would make a phone call. Then another would rush out and tell three others. Everybody in the area seemed to sense something big had happened. And by midnight the news was all over Nashville that Columbia Studios had just produced a record that could be a blockbuster.

This time I knew it was true. The more I listened to the playback, the more the goose bumps would form and the hair rise on my arms. I wanted to cry. I wanted to laugh.

Tom Hall (he added the "T" later, just as I added my "C") was sitting in Tootsie's Orchid Lounge that night, about a half mile from Columbia Studio, near Ryman Auditorium. Somebody ran all the way down to Tootsie's and told him what was going on. Tootsie's is legendary in Nashville. The walls are covered with photographs of country music's greatest stars — past and present — as well as people who have come and gone and are never thought of again. Tom was sitting at a table with red-checkered oilcloth when his friend burst in the door.

"You've got to hear what's happening down at Columbia," he shouted. And half the folks in Tootsie's took off for the studio. Like a lot of song writers, Tom was struggling to fight his way through the pack and reach the front, and when he heard the recording he knew, like all the rest of us, that he finally had a winner.

It was after midnight when I finally left the studio for home. By then Shelby Singleton had already told me I could use my real name on the label. "In fact," he consented, "we'll go a step further. You can use your middle initial. Remember Jaye P. Morgan? Well, you can be Jeannie C. Riley."

I liked the sound of it. The only thing he did different was add an "i" to Jeanne—so that everyone would know it was Jeannie and not Jean. From that time on I was Jeannie. I even sign my name that way.

It was 1 a.m. when I called Mama in Anson.

"Mama, I've just recorded a song that will be a number one hit in the nation."

"Oh, don't give me that," Mama said. I realized I had

wakened her, but it seemed too important to keep until morning.

"I mean it, Mama."

"Honey, you been writing me letters for nigh on two years saying that. What's different about this song?"

"It's just different, Mama. It's got magic. It's gonna sell a million records. Just you wait and see."

"Well, I sure hope so, baby," she said. Her voice sounded faint as if she was drifting off to sleep.

I hung up the phone and went in and looked at Kim, two and a half years old. She was asleep in her baby bed, her little pixie bangs sticking to her forehead. It was hard to believe we were so poor we couldn't afford air conditioning, and now we were about to become so rich. I reached down and touched her little gown, moist in the humid night.

"It's all gonna change, little baby," I whispered. "We're headed for the mountain top for sure now."

Saturday morning Shelby took the masters into the studio. The engineers mixed it and sent the final to the pressing plant. By Monday we had records. All day I sat in Jerry Chesnut's office and addressed handwritten notes, 200 of them, to disc jockeys across the land. They were to be mailed out with the records, telling them who I was, the name of the record, and why I thought this was going to be the biggest hit ever to ride to the top of the charts. Every time I mentioned "Harper Valley PTA" or my own name, I put down the black pen and wrote it in red. I wanted Jeannie C. Riley and "Harper Valley PTA" to leap out at the disc jockeys.

That night we airmailed copies across the nation. We did the same thing Tuesday night. On Wednesday the repercussions began bouncing back. It was as though an atomic bomb had been dropped on the nation.

I called Mama: "You know I told you the record would sell a million copies. Forget it. It's going to sell two million."

The disc jockeys went wild. One station in Ohio played the record 26 times in one day. A number of radio stations banned the record, it was so controversial. That just increased the sales at the record shops and music stores. It was as if the whole country came to a halt to listen to "Harper Valley PTA."

Thursday morning a young fellow, Larry Lee, who worked next door for Screen Gems, stopped by our office. He had a transistor radio pressed to his ear. Larry had been by the office a number of times. In fact, he often brought his sack lunch into my office to eat. But this time he stood in the doorway, the radio pressed to his ear, and said, "Wow, here's something you've got to hear!"

He held the radio to my ear.

"I know," I grinned. "That's me."

His eyes widened, and he got a strange look on his face. "You're kidding?" he said.

"No," I laughed. "I recorded it last Friday for Plantation Records."

He backed out of the office, his radio still pressed to his ear, never taking his eyes off me. Suddenly he broke and ran down the hall. Within minutes, it seemed, the sidewalk outside Jerry's office was filled with gawkers. The traffic in the hall was so thick the people could not even pass one another. It was as if the entire building had to get up and go to the bathroom at once—and everyone was parading outside my office.

How could it be? That little country girl with more twang in her voice than a Texas fiddle. The one with the orange fishnet hose, the navy blue skirt and orange and white shoes who bought her clothes from the discount department store for a dollar down and a dollar a week, the one with three inches of knee showing below her miniskirt, the one with the long floppy hair and pouty lip had just screamed to the top of every chart in the nation.

I loved it. I loved hearing them whisper, "I thought she was Rhonda Renae. Now she's Jeannie C. Riley." But it was a funny sensation. People like Larry Lee, whom I had known and laughed with and eaten lunch with, now stood at the end of the hall, peeking around the corner, as if I were the Queen of England—or Madam Frankenstein.

But what they thought didn't make any difference. I had become who I said I would become. Queen of the mountain. Look out, Connie; look out, Tammy; look out, Loretta. I'm here, too. Just as I said I would be.

My boss came in and said, "There's no sense you sticking around anymore." Jerry was grinning. "Your head's gonna be in the clouds anyway."

I felt guilty knowing I had promoted my record on his time. Even so, I walked out of Passkey Music with never a thought of returning.

That night I hand carried a copy of the record to WSM Radio in Nashville and gave it to Ralph Emery, one of the nation's most influential disc jockeys. Mickey went with me, and we hung around while he made his announcement over the air about my being in the studio. Instantly every phone in the building lit up as hundreds of people from all over the country called wanting to talk to me. Mickey grinned and stood over to one side, listening as I chattered into first one phone and then another.

On the way home that night, Mickey wanted to talk.

"Ralph Emery was acting like a preacher," he said.

"What do you mean?"

"He was saying things like, 'Y'all be really careful. So many families break up as soon as the singer hits the big time.'"

He looked over at me and took my hand in the seat beside him. "That ain't gonna happen to us, is it, honey?"

I patted his hand. "Don't you worry. Everything's gonna be just the same."

He gave me a long look. His face was so gaunt. His eyes, behind those little glasses, seemed to blink extra hard. He tightened his lips, then smiled slightly. "I reckon everyone has his troubles," he said. "I'd sure rather be troubled by having too much than by having too little."

"Me, too," I laughed. I was too excited to remember I no longer loved him.

Friday I was on my way to Philadelphia to do a big teen show for TV. I sang "Harper Valley PTA" to the sound track before a thousand screaming kids, and did "The Ballad of Louise" for an encore.

Mickey went along. So did Pete Terry and his wife. And a dozen other promotion-type people from Nashville. We stayed at the Marriott Hotel. Shelby Singleton had ordered all our meals, complete with champagne and huge tips. I didn't know it at the time, but he was paying for everything out of my profits. However, at that time it didn't make any difference. When you've had nothing and suddenly somebody hands you the world, you don't care if a few other people want to come along for the ride. We were living high.

That night Shelby talked about being clairvoyant, and suddenly I accepted it all. He was consulting with a psychic in California. In fact, he said, all that was happening to me had been destined in the stars. From the very beginning of time, he said, I had been preordained for this moment. It must be truth, I thought. He had promised a million seller, and it had come to pass. I had seen it with my own eyes. That night in Philadelphia I bought my first book on astrology.

Saturday we were in New York. I could hardly believe it. Here were Mickey and I walking down Fifth Avenue in early September. Shelby had given us an advance of several thousand dollars, more money than we had ever had at one time, and told me to buy some decent clothes. The only stage shoes I had were those little pointy-toed shoes Mama and I had bought at a factory outlet in Abilene before we moved to Nashville. But now pointy-toed shoes were out of style. So Mickey and I went into a big-name shoe store in New York, and I bought a pair of silver shoes and another pair of gold ones.

It was late afternoon when we headed back to the hotel. I had done Dick Clark's American Bandstand, live, and had another show that night. But the excitement seemed dulled because of Mickey. *This could be such a romantic place,* I thought, *if there was only someone here to enjoy it with— someone other than Mickey. If only he would talk or even hold my hand.* Pete and his wife were always talking and laughing. Mickey just sat there.

He didn't seem to notice my isolation and withdrawal. But suddenly he seemed to like the big time. That night in the hotel room he picked up the phone and dialed room service. Neither of us had ever used room service before in our lives. I wasn't sure what they did. But Mickey had everything under control.

"I don't care if it is after midnight," he snapped into the phone. "This is Jeannie C. Riley up here, and we want some food sent up—right now!"

And he got action.

I was embarrassed by changes I began to see in Mickey. His arrogance. His quick temper. I wanted him to be gentle and tender toward me. But he seemed to be moving in another direction.

The next week Mickey bought a huge diamond ring which he flashed around the service station and ordered a lavender-colored, custom Cadillac. He began going to Mister Mel to get his hair styled in a sprayed pompadour so he'd look like Conway Twitty and Porter Wagoner.

I was changing, too, of course, but I looked at my change as "growing up," while I condemned Mickey for "conforming."

The following week we were in Fort Lauderdale, Florida, with singer Waylon Jennings. That night after the performance the two of us were standing in the wings waiting for the final act to close.

"You won't stay married to that man very long," Waylon said seriously, looking across the stage where Mickey was leaning up against the wall smoking a cigarette. Mickey looked so out of place among these "genuine" entertainers. He had his hair fixed in that odd-looking pompadour, sprayed so it was rolled high over his forehead and fell back around his ears. He was dressed in an ill-fitting continental suit with a huge gold medallion hanging around his neck on a chain.

"He's probably a good old boy," Jennings said, "but he just don't fit the scene."

I looked up at Waylon, and he wasn't smiling. He was serious. Like everyone else who spoke with any kind of authority, I believed him.

That night I stayed awake thinking: *I wonder how much longer I can go on with Mickey?* I dreaded the thought of leaving him, but I felt Waylon had spoken as a prophet. It was inevitable. My wagon was hitched to a star, and Mickey was excess baggage. Yet what would happen if I told him to leave?

Outside I could hear the wind blowing in the palm trees and the sound of the surf far below as it crashed against the sandy beach. I walked out on the little balcony of our hotel room. The moonlight reflected off the dark green ocean and glistened in the surf as it broke in white shards in the shallows. If only I had a husband I could love. I would walk the beach with him and let the sand squiggle between my toes. I'd hold his hand and run, splashing in the warm surf. *I've inherited the kingdom of heaven, but I need the right man. I wonder who that's going to be?*

I thought of Pete Terry and his wife who had accompanied us to Florida, standing in front of the fancy hotel holding hands, waiting for the taxi. *If only I had someone like Pete. That's all I need to make all my dreams come true: someone I could feel love for.*

It was natural for me to gravitate to Pete—to tell him about my problems. He was quitting his job at the radio station and was going to manage me full time. There were so many career details, bookings, so much to do. I was with him constantly.

Mickey had quit his job at the service station less than a month after "Harper Valley PTA" was released. "My $90 a week is like spittin' in the ocean," he said. But it wasn't good for him to be without a job. He lost his motivation. Instead of being with me, he began hanging around bars and pool rooms, drinking Jack Daniels with the guys from Shelby Singleton's. What else was there for him to do? He had become Mr. Jeannie C. Riley. And what bothered me most was that he seemed to enjoy it.

But I didn't want someone like that for a husband. I wanted a man who cared, who would take authority, who would protect me and guide me. Mickey didn't seem to understand. So I turned to Pete.

Pete and I went to New Orleans where I was booked to do a TV show. Since a band wasn't involved we had the time to ourselves.

After a series of cocktails I sobbed out all my frustrations about Mickey. Here I was riding on a star, and he was still sitting under a haystack chewing a straw.

Soon Pete opened up and was sharing all his marital

problems with me. What I had thought was a fairyland marriage was as hypocritical as mine. Was everyone putting up a front? Were there any happy marriages any place?

He held my hand tightly that night. I needed someone to soothe me, someone like him with a disc jockey mentality— charming, congenial, easy with words. Mickey never talked, unless it was to ask for something or announce it was time for him to get to bed. But Pete was something else.

"You've gotta be mighty careful," Pete said. "There's a lot of folks who'll take advantage of you now that you're on top."

"I know," I sighed.

"I sure hope you don't have anything in your past or anyone in your past who's gonna appear and try to hurt you now that you're big time," he said.

"Don't worry," I mumbled, "I've lived a pretty dull life."

Then, suddenly, I remembered that evening on the sofa in Phil Blackman's apartment—and the flashing camera lights.

"Oh, my God!" I said, sitting up straight—my eyes wide open.

"What's wrong?" Pete asked, alarmed.

"Oh, my God!" I repeated. "There may be something."

"What is it?" Pete asked.

"I can't tell you. But there may be someone who has some pictures who could blackmail me."

"Oh, Lord," Pete groaned. "Tell me who it is."

"I can't," I said.

"Then whoever it is, you better do everything you can to get those pictures back. That's the kind of thing that could kill you. I mean, finish you for good."

9

Paying for Yesterday

Early Monday morning I was in my lavender Cadillac, hoping no one would recognize me, on my way to Black Rose Records. It was the first time I had seen Phil since he signed my "freedom papers." I was scared. All I could think about was coming home and finding Mickey standing in the living room, his face white, his hands shaking, holding an envelope full of pictures which Phil might have made that night in his apartment. Even worse, what if he threatened to send them to Mama and Daddy? I knew I had to get those pictures, somehow, some way.

Phil was packaging records when I walked in. He looked up, startled. Sheepish. The desk was covered with stacks of records and packing materials. I picked up one of the records. It was one of my songs I had recorded for the Black Rose label—which, at the time, he had said wasn't worth trying to sell.

"You skunk," I said, slamming the record down on the table. "Why didn't you try to sell this when it would have meant something to me?"

I could tell, just from watching his hands quivering, that he was afraid. "What do you mean?" he asked, his eyes never meeting mine. "I told you all along I was going to sell your records. It just wasn't the right time."

"Now you figure it's the right time," I said sarcastically. "After 'Harper Valley PTA.' "

"I don't understand," he said, continuing his packing, never letting his eyes come in contact with mine. "What's 'Harper Valley PTA'?"

"It's on every station in the country, and you know it."

He finally raised his eyes and looked at me. And suddenly I realized I was still vulnerable. I didn't want to look into his eyes. That spell was still there, and I was afraid of it. Terrified. This time I dropped mine.

He walked around from behind the table. "How are you, Jeannie?" he asked tenderly. "It's been so long since I've seen you. Despite all the trouble, I've never been able to get you off my mind. I . . ."

I interrupted him. My heart was pounding in my chest and I knew if I didn't speak my piece, I'd be like putty in his hands.

"I've come after those pictures," I said quickly.

"What pictures?"

"Those pictures you made in your apartment. You said you didn't have a camera. You said it was just a flash attachment, but I just don't believe you."

A tiny smile played over his handsome face and he ran his hand along the side of his greased ducktail, smoothing the hair away from his ears. "It will take me a couple of days," he said. "I don't have anything here at the office."

"I'll stop back on Wednesday," I said, relieved. "This means a lot to me."

Out on the sidewalk I began to shake. I knew I was walking on eggshells. I had to have those pictures back.

Early Wednesday morning I was in the Black Rose office, standing across the desk from Phil. "I want to put an end to this whole mess," I announced.

"Jeannie, no one wants to hurt you," Phil said kindly. "We had a lot of fun together, and I want to leave this with good memories. That's the reason I'll do whatever you say, just to keep you from being hurt."

"Do you really mean that?"

"Of course I mean it." He came around the desk and sat on the corner, close to where I was standing. I could smell that same familiar cologne and felt a wave of uneasiness sweep over me.

"I told you I would never hurt you," he said. Reaching behind him on the desk, he picked up a brown manila envelope. Tapping it gently with one finger, he held it for a moment, then laid it back on the desk. "See, this is proof that I won't hurt you. You asked me for something, and I'm willing to give it to you."

"Are those the pictures?" I asked, stepping back toward the chair. My mouth was dry, the palms of my hands moist. I wished I had brought someone with me. I tugged at my dress, wishing I had not worn such a short miniskirt.

"You asked me to get you the pictures, didn't you?" he asked. "What do you think is in the envelope?"

"I wasn't even sure there were pictures. You said that night you were just fooling around. But I have to know."

I could hardly believe what I was doing walking into the enemy camp and laying out my entire battle plan—for him to approve. How dumb! Naive!

"I'm glad you've come," he said. "And I really want to give you this envelope. Just to ease your mind. You're gonna be a great star, Jeannie, and you don't need any dark shadow from the past hanging over your head to harm you. That's the reason I want to get everything cleared up so we can go our separate ways and not hurt each other."

"That's the way I want it, Phil."

"There's one more thing we need to do," Blackman said. He had a sheet of paper in his hand. The thought flashed through my head: *Be careful. This is no man to fool with.*

"You know I'm releasing a record on you." He gestured toward a stack of records and mailers in the corner. "But I've lost our original contract. Remember you were writing for the Blackman Music Company and recording for Black Rose. Of course all that was under my parent corporation in New York."

I was lost. I never had been able to understand stuff like that. All I knew was he had signed a release so I didn't have to do any more records for Black Rose. What had happened before that was incidental. Why was he now bringing it all up?

He saw the puzzled look on my face and continued. "I've got to have proof that you were recording for me back then. Otherwise, if I put this record out, you could sue me, saying I didn't have any right to release it."

"Why would I want to sue you?" I asked. "What I did back then was yours. You have every right to put out my record. I just wish you'd done it back then, when it could have helped me more."

He dropped his eyes. "I lied to you the other day," he said. "I knew what had happened to you. Things have not been going very well around here. I was determined to honor the release I gave you, but when you hit it big with Plantation, I suddenly saw a chance. It might be my only chance. So I've got your early songs on record, and maybe I can sell enough of them to keep from going under. Of course you'll get your royalties ..."

"Why didn't you tell me this the other day instead of lying?"

"I had lost your contract, and I was afraid you'd try to stop me. And Jeannie ..." his voice broke and he hung his head again, "this might be my last chance."

"What do you want me to do?" I asked, feeling sorry for him.

"I have drawn up another contract. It's just the same as the one you had with us before. I've backdated it so it will be legitimate. If you'll sign it, that will give me the legal right to publish the four songs you did for me before you got big."

Everything in me said, *Don't do it. Wait. Have it checked by an attorney.* But how could I do that without exposing my situation with Phil? He had the pictures. If I delayed he might not give them to me.

So I signed, thinking I was doing this one last thing to help him out. And I could see the back date on the contract.

He folded the contract, walked around his desk, put it in the top drawer of his desk and picked up the brown manila envelope.

"These are yours," he said softly.

"I don't want to see them," I said, backing off.

He looked startled. "I don't understand. I thought that's

what you came for."

I didn't want to look. It was a strange self-deception. If I didn't look at the pictures it was almost as if they might not really be there.

I thought back to my childhood. If Mama said, "Jeannie, don't ride your bicycle across the street to Susanne's," I would obey the letter of her law. But I thought nothing of riding my bike to the highway, walking it across, so I could get to Susanne's house from the other side. That way I could justify what I was doing.

"I want to burn the past," I said. "I'm sick of it. I want to be free. I want you to burn them. Now. Right here."

"You don't even want to look in the envelope? How do you know I'm not tricking you? How do you know whether there are any pictures or not?"

"You wouldn't go through all this if there weren't pictures in that envelope. I'll be happy if you'll just burn the envelope right now."

There was a slight smile on his face as he reached in his desk drawer and pulled out a pack of matches. Striking one, he held it under the corner of the manila envelope until it began to flame. Then he put it in his trash basket and allowed it to burn. I wanted to watch. I wanted to know if there were any pictures—or negatives—in the envelope. But I didn't. I sat in the chair with my eyes closed until the envelope was entirely consumed. Phil opened the window and let the smoke clear, then looked back at me.

"Satisfied?"

I nodded. And hoped.

Out in the parking lot I sat in the front seat of my car, thinking. *Did I do the right thing? It all seemed too easy.* I put the key in the ignition and started to back out. When I did, I glanced in my rear view mirror and saw Phil and his secretary in a mad run from his office across the back of the parking lot toward his car. Suddenly I had a deep sinking feeling in the pit of my stomach.

It took me 30 minutes to drive home. Mickey had come in for lunch and met me at the door.

"Have you heard the radio?" he asked.

I just stared at him.

"It was on the news just now. Black Rose Records has just announced they're suing you for $400,000 for breach of contract."

I couldn't breathe. He had it planned all along. He had baited the hook, dangled it in front of me, and I had gulped it down. He even had the news release to the radio station prepared so he could get instant publicity. I staggered in and leaned against the kitchen counter. What had gone wrong? I had my release from Blackman Music Company saying as an artist I was free to go. The backdated contract I had just signed shouldn't affect that. But I hadn't even read what I had just signed. *Oh, God, what have I done?*

Without saying anything to Mickey, I bolted and ran. Out the back door toward the car.

"Hey, where are you going? Where have you been?" He stood in the door watching as I screeched the tires of the car.

"I'll be back later. I've got to stop this before it goes any further."

But I knew it was too late. Still I drove like a wild woman, heading up the highway toward the radio station where Pete Terry was finishing his last week. But the damage had already been done. I had signed a contract that put me back under obligation to Phil Blackman's parent company. The release he signed was only from one small area of the big company. That meant I was back under contract to Blackman—and he was going to make me pay big.

I was half blind from the tears which were stinging my eyes. I pounded the steering wheel, screaming at the top of my voice as I swerved in and out of traffic. I turned sharply off the highway across the railroad tracks, then without looking, I spun the wheel to the left and swerved up the side road. I did not hear the shrill whistle of the thundering locomotive which came around the turn on the right side of the car and hurtled toward me.

It all happened so fast I was not even aware of how close it was. The train loomed over me as I roared across the tracks, missing my back bumper by less than a foot. The vacuum created by the rushing locomotive and the rumbling wheels almost flipped over my car. The screeching whistle faded down the tracks as I finally hit the brakes and sat, staring straight ahead, cold sweat pouring from my face. I was nauseated but too frightened to throw up. Had I been two seconds slower I would have been dead.

There was no time to be paralyzed with fear. I raced into the studio, looking for Pete. He was on the air but through the glass window saw me coming and quickly put on a long play record. He met me in the office. I was too angry to be cautious—or modest. I vomited out the entire Phil Blackman episode, my words tumbling over one another as I told him about the pictures, the scene in his office, the new contract.

"That _____!" Terry muttered. Then he said it louder and slammed his fist against the wall.

"I've gotta do something," I said, starting out the door.

"Hey, wait a minute. Where are you going?"

"I'm going to see Blackman and get that contract back."

"Listen, you've made enough of a mess of things. Leave it alone until we can talk to a lawyer."

"There's no time."

"I can't go with you," Pete shouted as I headed down the hall to the parking lot. "At least wait until I'm off work."

But I was already through the door—heading for Black Rose Records.

"You can't go in there," Phil's secretary said, jumping up from behind her desk as I pushed past.

"Try and stop me," I snapped.

She recoiled. "But he's got someone with him," she wailed as I slammed open the door to Phil's office and burst in.

"I'm here for that contract, Mr. S.O.B.," I shouted. "Give it to me now or I'll tear this place apart."

I didn't even notice the older man who was sitting in the chair talking to Blackman. I had but one thing in mind. To get that contract and tear it up.

Phil jumped up from his chair. "What do you think you're doing?" he shouted, as I started scattering papers on his desk, throwing books around, looking for the contract. "Can't you see I've got someone in here?"

"I don't care if you're talking to God Himself. You've deceived me for the last time, you filthy scum."

"What are you talking about?" Blackman said, trying to grab my hand.

"I'm talking about that contract I signed this morning. I want it back, and I want it back now." I grabbed books off his desk and threw them against the wall and finally got around behind where I could pull out his middle drawer where I had seen him put it.

We were struggling physically by now. The older man, whoever he was, had fled. Phil was trying to pin my arms. I was kicking, pulling at the drawer trying to get it out of the desk. Stuff was all over the carpet. His trash had overturned. The telephone crashed to the floor.

"Let's get out of here where we can talk," he said, glancing at his secretary who was standing in the door, dumbfounded.

"You just don't want her to know what we were up to, do you?" I screamed. Then I turned to her. "What's wrong, didn't he tell you about us?"

Her face blanched, and the lines around her mouth grew tight.

"That's enough, Jeannie," Phil said. He grabbed me and pulled me toward the door.

"I'm not leaving until you give me that contract," I screamed.

We were struggling, but somehow he managed to pull me through a little storage room and out onto a small porch behind his office. Then he grabbed me firmly by the shoulders.

"You cheap little slut," he said. "I was the first to take you in. I'm the only one who tried to do anything for you. Now you've lucked into a million dollar hit, and I'm gonna get a piece of it, one way or the other. You can't spit on me and get away with it."

"You think I can't!"

And I spit on him. I had never spit on anyone before, but I spit directly into his face. Then, crying, I ran around the side of the building to where I had double-parked in front of his office.

The next thing I remember is lying on the sofa at Kinda-Mama's house, while she rubbed my back and gave me a sedative. She called Mickey, but before he arrived I had told her everything. All the emotions—fear, loneliness, depression, anxiety—swept over me in great waves. And when I broke the story to Kinda-Mama, she just sat there, shaking her head.

"I wish I had known," she said sadly. "I could have been a friend to you. Why didn't you tell me?"

"I feel so lost," I said. "Isn't there anything that's real anymore? Is there anyone, anything I can lean on that won't move away? It seems that everything nailed down is coming loose, and I'm being swept along in the darkness."

"We're all that way," Kinda-Mama said softly. "It's just that some folks ain't as bad as others. But there ain't nobody good. I mean really good. Except Jesus."

Mickey finally took me home about midnight. We didn't talk. We never did. He was as lost as I. I cried myself to sleep that night, my back turned toward him. I had lost everything else that I ever wanted, so why try to make something out of my marriage? It, too, was finished. I'd just have to wait until Mickey found it out, too.

The next day I had to break the story to Shelby Singleton. Pete was in the office, listening, as I told them the entire, sordid mess.

"How could you do this to Shelby?" Pete moaned. "Why did you sign that paper?"

He was pounding the wall again, and everyone was calling everyone else an S.O.B. Finally he said, "Well, at least we'll know how to fight him. He thinks you won't tell. But we'll fight him on his own ground. And he won't fight back, because his wife and family live here in Nashville."

I hadn't even thought about that. But I was being read the ground rules. If a man strikes you on one cheek, you not only hit him back, but you kick him in the groin and then stab him in the back after he falls. That's the way the game is played—and I just wasn't dirty enough to have found that out in the first inning.

Shelby talked to Mickey, explaining he needed him to help set up a tour in the Midwest. Besides, he told him, it would be better if Mickey were not present for the trial. He wanted everything cool in the courtroom. They wanted me to look like the innocent girl under duress. Mickey might lose his temper. He agreed not to be there.

As it turned out, I didn't have to testify very much. Phil's wife and secretary came to the hearing, and as a result his lawyer was afraid to ask me any questions which might reveal our relationship. All I had to do was give short answers which left lots of questions. In the end, the judge threw the suit out of court since it was obvious that I had been deceived into the contract. Shelby's expensive attorneys had some tests run on my signature which proved it was fresher than the original signature. This, plus the fact the signature had not been witnessed, made the entire suit invalid.

I won, but it cost $33,000 in attorney's fees. I thought Shelby was paying for part of it, since Phil was not only suing me but was suing Plantation Records as well. It was not until much later that I discovered that every expense—all those expensive trips around the nation on the promotion tours, all the dinners, all the court costs, everything—was being deducted from my royalties.

The publicity of the case, however, increased the popularity of "Harper Valley PTA." My bookings increased. I was wanted everywhere.

10

Flying High

My fee for the week at the Las Vegas Flamingo Hotel was $30,000. When Elvis Presley made a special trip backstage after my opening night to wish me well, the photographers were called in. How I loved it!

Exactly why any night club would pay me this much for what I did still mystifies me. I opened with "Harper Valley PTA," did a few country standards, then danced a soft shoe and twirled a cane to a Dixieland medley.

Pete Terry had hired a choreographer who charged $10,000 for teaching me the few dance steps I did. I had learned to twirl a baton as a majorette in the Anson High School band. There were six dancers, four boys and two girls. A full orchestra, and my own guitar player, Ron Salmon. Pete helped me put together a back-up group called the Harper Valley PTA (what else?). They did a little singing and guitar playing along with the orchestra.

The third night I twirled my cane right out into the audience. It bounded off a table, hit a cocktail glass and spilled liquor over a half-drunk lady.

I saved the act by saying in saucy baby talk, "Oh, please don't sue me."

Most knew about the court case in Nashville and broke into laughter. It sounded so good I committed the unpardonable stage sin and did my line all over again, this time getting down on one knee to plead: "Oh, *please* don't sue me."

For months I was gone almost every night, traveling across the nation. Jimmy Key of Key Talent handled my bookings and did a good job lining up engagements. Jimmy had been at Columbia Studio the night I recorded "Harper Valley PTA" and sensed right away it was going to be a big hit. Only Jimmy didn't know just how big. As a result, he booked a number of one-night stands all over the nation at a fraction of what we could have gotten. Some of these were $300 a night, plus expenses. It seemed strange to go to one town for $300 a night and then to the next city and do the same show for $5,000. The bigger dates, those paying $3,000, $4,000 and $5,000 a night, did not come until after it was obvious that "Harper Valley PTA" was not a freak but would stay at the top of the charts for a long time.

I sang in auditoriums, clubs, honky-tonks, ballrooms, cow palaces and dance halls. The people would dance to the house band and then come and listen while I ran through my little repertoire ending with a rousing rendition of "Harper Valley PTA." I also played amusement parks and state fairs. They had to close the gates to Lake Winnepesaukah near Chattanooga not long after "Harper Valley" was out. They had their biggest crowd in history, more than 85,000. That, ironically, was one of those engagements where I got paid $500 since it had been booked before I was classed as a superstar.

I did "Hollywood Palace" less than a month after "Harper Valley" was out. I was on stage with Bing Crosby and Bobby Goldsboro and then came back for a second appearance on "Hollywood Palace" a month later with Roy Rogers and Dale Evans. Two months later I did a show with George Gobel. When I did the Ed Sullivan Show, I was so green I didn't even have enough sense to be nervous. The show was live and played to 30 million viewers.

I did all the big talk shows of the era and even a White House press conference with President Nixon in Washington. I sang and twirled the baton on Johnny Carson's "Tonight Show" and came back for two other appearances. I wanted to believe the folks had come out to hear me, but deep inside I knew it was the sock-it-to-'em satisfaction of "Harper Valley PTA" which drew them. The applause was thunderous when I was introduced as "the Harper Valley PTA girl." But it was the song, not me, which was important.

The biggest thrill of all was being invited back to Anson, Texas, in April 1969, for "Jeannie C. Riley Day." Governor Preston Smith was there. It fulfilled that dream I had often had as a child—entering a big room where the entire town had turned out in my honor. Here are portions from an article which appeared in the Sunday magazine, *Tempo,* distributed by the *Houston Post:*

> Well, sir, you wouldn't believe so many people would be out at the Abilene Municipal Airport so early in the morning. It isn't even 9 a.m. and still they come, driving slowly into the parking lot and looking for an empty spot, hurrying through the clean, compact terminal, crowding by the cyclone fence and the gate leading to the taxi strip . . .
>
> The aircraft stops, the door is opened and two men jump out, turning quickly to offer helping hands to the next passenger. It's Jeannie C. She's wearing a scarlet cape over a stunning white mini-miniskirted dress, scarlet net hose, scarlet mod boots. Everybody cheers and whistles and applauds. The 69-member band strikes up "I Dream of Jeannie With the Light Brown Hair."
>
> It's the Great American Dream. The little girl who leaves home to go out into the big world in search of fame and fortune; she finds them and returns triumphantly to red roses, cheers, tears, the embraces of family and friends. Over and over you hear, "I knew you could do it, Jeannie C."
>
> Only a few months of fame, and already Jeannie C. seems born to the purple. She graciously accepts the red roses, lifts an arm to wave to the throng . . .

"Born to the purple". . . " the Great American Dream." I ate it all up. It didn't bother me that it was 19 paragraphs into the story before the writer mentioned that Mickey was along also.

> In the big limousine with Jeannie C. is her husband,
> wafer-thin Mickey Riley. Here is another part of the
> Great American Dream: Boy and girl attend grade
> school together, then junior and senior high, fall in
> love and marry . . .

The only other reference to Mickey was that he stood in
the background "with his hands in his pants pockets which
isn't easy because his pants are quite snug."

Good old faithful Mickey. He had relaxed since the first
weeks of my success and stopped trying to take charge of
situations he didn't understand. Now he was just trying to
watch out for me. When someone asked me what he did
for a living, I introduced him as an astrologer.

"What's that mean?" the woman asked.

"Ask him," I giggled.

"That's right," Mickey said, blinking his eyes behind his
dark-rimmed glasses. "Just call me a stargazer. I gaze upon
my wife, the star."

They loved it. And so did I.

That night Governor Smith made a speech in which he
said, "Since 'Harper Valley PTA,' all attendance records at
PTA meetings have soared, members being afraid NOT to
go."

I was sitting beside him on the platform and saw his
notes. Where that line came, his speech writer had marked
in the margin: "Pause for applause and/or laughter."

The governor got both.

The benediction on the program was listed under "En-
tertainment." But so was everything else.

When a TV reporter asked what it was like to be famous,
I said, "I have no private life. I owe myself to the world."

Those around me, the people I was counting on most,
seemed to feel I owed myself mostly to them. Shelby kept
putting money into my account, but he also kept spending
my royalty money for expenses. Convinced that I needed to
be closer to town, he sent out a moving van and moved
us from our apartment in Madison to another on Harding
Place, at my expense.

When I got my first royalty statement, I discovered the expenses deducted were enormous: The lavender-colored Cadillac, all those flashy clothes, the huge hotel expenses for the large group that Shelby and Pete felt should travel with me, all their phone calls, their car expenses, their meals out and their drinks—gallons of drinks.

It was the eating out that got to me, for I was always expected to pay the bill. Actually Shelby would pay the bill, leave a huge tip—and later it would all show up on my expense account to be deducted from my royalties.

One of the girls at that time in bookkeeping told me that when she would carry the expense sheet to Shelby for the charge-backs, he would look at it and say, "Not enough charge-backs. Go dig up some more." She told me they were charging pencils, erasers, newspapers, magazines, anything they could come up with to my account. It was all legal, but I felt "took."

"Harper Valley PTA" sold more than three million copies in the first six months. But when my royalty check came at the end of the year, it amounted to a little less than $76,000. I had sold a million copies of the single, a million records of the album and had the second gold tape cartridge in history—signifying another million sales. In the year that followed, they sold multiple golden records in the millions. After the second royalty statement, which was less, I wasn't paid for another 10 years until we worked out a settlement for $20,000. Shelby always claimed there just wasn't enough money. Even so, when I considered the one-night stands, Mickey and I took in well over half a million dollars that first year.

The man I was looking to for help, Pete Terry, just wasn't equipped to handle what was going on. One day he was a deejay at a radio station, spinning records, and the next day he was supposed to fill the role of big-time manager. He was out of his class. And so was I.

Pete Terry got 15 percent of all my earnings. He had quit the radio station and rented an office in the Capitol Building on 16th Avenue—at my expense, of course. The booking agent got 10 percent of everything earned on the road. Shelby was getting five percent for "handling my finances."

Then he charged me another five percent for running my fan club.

We were living like royalty. Daddy took a leave of absence from his job so he and Mama could fly out and be with me whenever I wanted. He was the best mechanic in Anson and could go back whenever he chose, but he and Mama wanted to be with me. They would often meet me at various places where I was performing and fly back home.

Kim, who was almost three, would stay with my parents or the Rileys in Texas. Sometimes Mama and Daddy would fly to Nashville to take care of her for me. Since I found so little time to spend with her, guilt was forever strumming a plaintive song on the strings of my heart.

I missed, it seemed, all those important "firsts" in her life such as drawing her first picture or her first ride on her tricycle. I was always gone, caught up in the mad chase of an elusive phantom: fame.

One night I called Kim from Portland, Oregon, and spent more than two hours talking—just talking baby talk to her about silly things. When I hung up I spent the next hour with my face buried in the pillow of my lonely motel bed— sobbing. I was number one on the charts and last in the hearts of my family.

One evening after a show I called Mama and told her how homesick I was for her and Kim.

"She's doing just fine," Mama said. "Last night she saw you on the TV, and she ran up and hugged the set."

That made me feel even worse. I was a television mother.

When Mama would take her to the Super Dog for lunch, Kim would run over and kiss the juke box where my songs were played. Everyone else thought it was cute. But my heart was bleeding.

Then we went to England on a tour. In London Shelby and his wife, Mickey and I and some of the key people in the firm that was handling my records in England, went out one night. We were using a car formerly owned by the Beatles and had gone to several of the swanky night places in London, winding up at a discotheque which was the hangout for the Beatles.

The star salesman, a large man with glasses and slicked-back hair kept leaning over the table asking me to dance. I was afraid of him and didn't want to dance with him; but he kept insisting. Shelby kept poking me, whispering, "Go ahead and dance with him. Go ahead."

"Look, she don't want to dance!" Mickey blurted out.

Every head turned and looked at Mickey. His face was red, and his Irish temper was up. "Y'all leave her alone. You're pushing her too much!"

"Well, our friend here wants to dance with her, and he has every right to ask," Shelby said. "I don't see why she won't dance with him. Besides, it's just good business."

"Business, hell," Mickey snorted. "Is that all you ever think about? Jeannie don't have to dance with nobody, business or not."

I was embarrassed for Mickey yet proud of him. He wasn't intimidated by anyone. Faithful. Loyal. And ready to fight for me if he had to.

Suddenly the salesman leaned across the table, grabbed my hand, and almost yanked me out of my seat. "Let's dance," he said rudely.

That was it for Mickey. He jumped to his feet, turned over his chair and grabbed the man's wrist. "Buddy, this is the last time. Now don't ask her again. The lady don't want to dance." Mickey had his other hand doubled into a fist.

The big man softened and gently reached up and took Mickey's hand, the one wrapped around his wrist. "I understand, old chap," he said, smiling sweetly at Mickey. "Then why don't *you* dance with me? I go both ways, you know."

Mickey turned pale and shook his hand loose as though it were a snake wrapped around his wrist. He backed off, looking first at the distributor, then at Shelby. Shelby just shrugged his shoulders at Mickey and said, "Whatever turns you on."

"Well, that don't turn me on one bit," Mickey snapped.

"As you wish," the big man said. He left the table and headed toward another man standing near the bar. Moments later they were not only dancing but kissing mouth to mouth.

"Man, I gotta get out of here," Mickey said, looking wildly for the exit. "This ain't no place for a Texas cowboy."

"We can't leave our host," Shelby said, irritated.

"I gotta go to the bathroom," Mickey said. "And he better be ready to leave when I get back, or we're leaving without him."

Minutes later Mickey came rushing out of the restroom his eyes wide. "You won't believe what happened in there," he gasped. "There's a man standing in the middle of the room wearing a tuxedo with a towel draped over his arm. When I stepped up to the urinal, he moved to my side. When I tried to push him away, he said, 'I'm here to assist you. There's no need for you to dirty your hands.' I told him, 'Buddy, where I come from, a man does this sort of thing by himself.'

"He backed up like I hurt his feelings or something. But when I finished and headed to the sink to wash my hands, why dadgum, he beat me to it. He even turned on the water for me. I washed my hands and looked for a towel but there weren't none. Then this dude takes the towel off his arm. I started to reach for it, but he pulled it back and said, 'I'll dry, sir!' By golly, that dude dried my hands for me."

Shelby was laughing. "You mean there's a man in there who unzips your britches?"

"I don't believe that," I said.

"You want to see for yourself?" Mickey asked. "Come on. Everything goes around here."

I got up to go see.

Mickey went in first, then waved me in. Sure enough, there was a funny little man standing in the middle of the room wearing a tux with a towel over his arm.

"Are you really here for what they said you were here for?" I gulped.

He gave me a strange look and stepped back toward one of the stalls. "Madam," he said with a serious look on his face, "this is a men's room."

Mickey had had enough and insisted we leave. But that night at the hotel he began to argue with me about my "friends." We had already ordered sandwiches from room service when the fight began.

"Listen, they aren't my friends," I said. "They're just business associates. I don't like 'em any more than you."

"Then how come you've got 'em all on the payroll?" Mickey shouted. "It looks like we're supporting half the music industry."

"I can't help it," I shouted back. "We've got enough money for everyone and more than enough for us, too."

"I'm tired of supporting a bunch of freaks and panhandlers," Mickey said. "Where I come from a man works for his living; he don't live off someone else. That's called 'hustling,' not working. And I sure ain't no hustler."

Annoyed, I picked up a brown paper sack in which Mickey carried our cash. The sack was filled with $50 and $100 bills—more than $30,000 worth. I was still yelling. "You're so cheap you won't even use a bank. You act like you're still living in the backwoods, carrying all this money around in a grocery sack. What do you know about money? And what right do you have to criticize my friends?"

"I thought they weren't your friends," Mickey shouted, his face scarlet. He grabbed the grocery sack from me, ripping its side. Some of the money fell on the floor.

"Pick it up," I screamed, livid with rage. "It may not mean anything to you, but it sure means something to me."

"Then you pick it up," Mickey hollered. I stuck my chin in the air, defiantly. He bent over and grabbed a handful of bills out of the sack. "But if it means so much to you, then here it is!"

He threw it at me. The bills fluttered around the room.

Suddenly we were in it, screaming, cussing and flinging money about. Each of us grabbed handfuls of bills—$20's, $50's, $100's—and threw them wildly all over the room. They fell like leaves on an autumn day in the mountains of Tennessee. They were on the bed, on the dresser, sticking to the lampshades, scattered all over the carpet—$30,000 worth of bills.

Suddenly there was a knock at the door. Before we could do anything, we heard a key in the lock and the door opened. There stood a very prim looking maid, dressed in black with a white pinafore. She was pushing a little wagon with the room service food. She barely got in the door when she spotted the money. It was every place. She looked up at us, our faces still red from the shouting and cussing. "H-h-here's your f-f-food, mum," she stuttered. She quickly backed out, leaving the door open as she ran down the hall toward the elevator.

Moments later Shelby was in the room. "I could hear you shouting down at the end of the hall," he said.

Then he saw the money. "Great God in heaven," he stammered. "What's going on here?" Without another word he started picking up the money and putting it back in the torn paper sack.

"It's been a bad night," he said, putting the sack on the dresser. "Why don't you all get some sleep, and we'll talk in the morning."

Shelby did talk but not to Mickey—only to me.

"Mickey's gotta go," he said. "We've got too big a thing going for him to mess it up."

"Well, what can I do with him?" I said. "I can't tell him to ship off to Texas."

"I don't mean that," Shelby said. "I like Mickey. He's got guts and he's real. But he's gonna ruin us if he stays with you on tour. We can't afford to have him make some disc jockey angry. And if some record producer wants to put his arm around you or have a friendly dance, we can't have Mickey along raising hell like he did last night."

"Well, Mickey sure ain't much for patting people on the back and smiling sweet when he don't feel like it," I admitted.

"That's right," Shelby agreed. "You're just beginning, baby, and you don't need no filling station cowboy to hold you back. We're selling sexiness and sauciness. He's a good old boy but too homespun for us."

I didn't like the image he painted of me. The photographers were always saying, "Hike your skirt" . . . "Lift your eyebrow" . . . "Pout a little bit." They were building a "Harper Valley PTA image." But deep inside I felt that the real person was buried behind my miniskirt and boots. In the long run I felt the sex symbol would destroy me. I was number one in the nation now, but just below the horizon was someone else with another hit song who would take my place. I was alive as long as my song lived.

The first year they televised the Country Music Association awards at Ryman Auditorium, I had been nominated as female vocalist of the year, for record of the year, and "Harper Valley PTA" had been nominated for song of the year. It was to have been the biggest night of my life.

I had asked Elsie of Nashville, a leading dress designer, to make my dress for the awards ceremony. Mama was going to be with me in Nashville, and I wanted to do something that would impress her. It was the night I had dreamed of, with Mama sitting on the front row. I was determined to break the typecast of me as always wearing a miniskirt with fishnet hose and high boots. I sat down with Elsie, and we designed the dress together. It was to be a blue velvet top with old-fashioned, puff-type sleeves that continued down the arm with long rows of old-fashioned covered buttons. It was to have a little scoop neckline with an empire waist. Then, under the bust and continuing all the way to the floor, was to be layer after layer of organza. The craze for old-fashioned clothes was just coming in, and I wanted to be a model for the way a country girl should look. The idea of Loretta Lynn being a genuine country girl, who appealed to wives as well as husbands, appealed to me also. But if Loretta was the girl next door, I was portrayed as the saucy tramp from the other side of the tracks. That was the Shelby Singleton image that I wanted to change.

The afternoon of the awards I rushed by Elsie's to pick up my dress. When she spread it out, I was stunned. The top was just as we had planned, complete with puff sleeves at the shoulder and long buttoned glove sleeves to the wrist. But what had been planned as an old-fashioned, full skirt with many layers of organza had been chopped off into a miniskirt with only three layers of organza ending almost 10 inches above my knee.

I stood and stared, unbelieving. "What's that?" I finally choked out.

"Well, hon," she said nervously, "now listen to this and

try to understand."

"Understand what?" I shouted. "What have you done to my dress?"

"I had the dress all finished, and it was one of the most beautiful things I've ever done," she said apologetically. "But Shelby Singleton called this morning. He said, 'If Jeannie shows up at the awards tonight in anything but a miniskirt, you'll never sew another thing for her.' I felt I didn't have any choice but to cut it off into a miniskirt."

"Shelby Singleton's not paying for this dress!" I shouted. "I am! What right do you have to accept orders from him about what I'm to wear? There's no way I'll wear that freaky dress. It'll make me look like a stork."

Elsie shook her head. "Listen, Jeannie, you don't really call the shots in a deal like this. Shelby does. I thought you knew that by now."

I was fighting off the tears. "Isn't there any place where I can be my own boss and make my own decisions?"

When I got home I called Shelby and stormed at him. "Pick out some silver boots," he said calmly. "The crowd will love it."

"You don't have any right to tell me what to wear," I said. "This is my night. I have a right to wear what I want."

"You don't understand," Shelby said patiently. " 'Harper Valley PTA' just can't be sung by a girl in a long dress. The world knows you as a sassy, sexy, sock-it-to-'em girl. If you show up in an old-fashioned dress, it will kill the whole thing."

"I'm not Miss Harper Valley PTA, you know," I shot back. "I'm an artist and I have a right to . . . "

He broke me off. "You're not an artist, baby. You're a commodity—a miniskirted, silver-booted commodity. Now be there early. We've got a show to rehearse." And he hung up.

I went to my room, fell across my bed and cried.

There was more hurt yet to come. Shelby had never liked my mother. He said I changed when she came around, pretended to be something I was not. He tolerated Mickey simply because I was married to him. But when it came to Mama, he told me on several occasions that she was in the way. He knew she disapproved of my short skirts, the sexy motions and the suggestive lyrics to the songs he wanted me to sing. To him, she represented old-fashioned, fundamental Christianity. Even though he didn't mind me or any of his singers using gospel lyrics ("It's good business, sweetheart. Tug at them heart strings and they'll buy records."), in his business it seemed to me he was opposed to the application of any of the gospel ethics. He believed that we all should set our own standards. So when it came to Mama, he felt she influenced me and made me ineffective in the world where he wanted me to star. For that reason he had not gotten her a ticket to attend the awards.

Mama had always dreamed of being a country music star. She loved the music. When I made it big, no one in the entire world was more pleased than Mama. It was even better than if it had happened to her. Mama just knew I was going to win something. To be nominated in three categories almost assured me of a win in at least one of them.

Although Ryman Auditorium was sold out, and everybody in the music industry was trying to get tickets, I just assumed that Shelby would take care of Mama as well as Mickey. But Shelby avoided me all afternoon, and in the hustle and bustle of the rehearsals, dressing and makeup I neglected to call Mama until several hours before the program was to start.

"Did anybody get you a ticket?" I screamed over the noise in the backstage area.

I could barely hear her, but I knew she was crying.

"What's the matter? Why aren't you coming?" I shouted into the phone.

"Someone needs to stay with Kim." She said something about watching the awards on TV. I told Mama I loved her and hung up.

I wanted to bang my hand against the phone booth. It was all wrong. My mother should be here for the awards on this most special night of my life.

Everything was going wrong. I felt that I looked like a flamingo in my dress. I almost wished I didn't have to be called to the stage. Tammy Wynette won female vocalist of the year. Song of the year was "Little Green Apples." And "Harper Valley PTA" won record of the year. They called me to the stage and the orchestra went into my introduction. There I was, with my freaky dress—half formal, half miniskirt—with my skinny legs protruding into those silver boots, standing with all the rest of Nashville royalty who were dressed in formal attire, belting out "Harper Valley PTA."

I had trouble concentrating. I kept noticing Lynn Anderson, sitting on the front row, laughing and punching her husband. Dumb me. I didn't know that they and a thousand other people were making fun of my costume. There I stood—big flowing skirt at the waist, cut off at the pantie line, with two little legs sticking out underneath. It was supposed to have been a French Marie Antoinette. Instead it was a Nashville ostrich.

After the awards program was over and the people were filing out of the giant auditorium, they called all the award winners to the platform to have their pictures taken. I was embarassed, standing between Johnny Cash and Porter Wagoner who was with Dolly Parton. Then there was Glen Campbell, Bobby Russell and Chet Atkins—all holding awards and dressed in formal clothes while I stood there with my knees sticking out, feeling more awkward than I had ever felt in my life.

All I could think about was my poor Mama. She had wanted to come so badly. I just stood there, feeling awful.

Flashbulbs were going off all over the stage when in the middle of the commotion I heard a tiny voice, which I would have recognized even from hell, calling out from the darkness of the back balcony.

"Mommy! Mommy!"

It was Kim. I ran forward to the edge of the stage, staring at the back of the theatre. For a fleeting second I saw them there, high in those dark seats. There was the image of Mama's horrified face, distraught that I had discovered them. And little Kim in her arms, her arms outstretched toward me.

Somehow they had gotten there. But how? I waved at them and frantically shouted: "Mama!"

"Jeannie, we're not finished with the pictures." It was Shelby's voice. He steered me back to the group.

I stepped back in beside Johnny Cash. The flashbulbs started all over again. But all I could see was Mama in her old everyday clothes high in that balcony. Embarrassed by the outburst, she was holding her hand over Kim's mouth as they hurried out of the theatre.

In my hand I had one of the most coveted Music City awards. I was in the line-up with the superstars of music. My records had already sold millions of copies, and my name was on the lips of more than 100 million Americans— and it was all empty. I was 22 years old, and I felt like I was 80.

Mickey drove us home. I didn't even try to tell him what was wrong. It was long after midnight when we reached the house. I fell across my bed in tears.

Mama sat on the edge of the bed trying to comfort me. She had called Pete Terry, and he had gotten her the ticket. Then she rode downtown in a cab.

"Jeannie, I don't understand," she said. "This is a dream come true for you."

Poor Mama. She was so simple. So uncomplicated. She didn't understand how empty material things were, for she never had acquired them.

"Mama, I've given them everything. I've practiced three and four hours a day singing into that tape recorder. Now I feel like a sponge gone dry. I've been squeezed until there's nothing left. It's a fearful feeling, Mama. I could die tonight, and they would forget me tomorrow. I've left nothing behind."

"Poor baby," Mama said, rubbing my back. "Ain't no reason to feel that way. You got us. What more could you want?"

"Mama, I've got none of you. There's a 'they' out there that has control of me. If you don't please them, you're lost. I want to sing country music. I want to do something deeper, something that has meaning, something that might even change people's lives—and all they will let me do is trash. I've got my star, Mama, but it's made out of yesterday's wadded-up newspaper."

Jeannie and her sister, Helen, in 1947 when Jeannie was 2
years old. Helen was 6.

Oscar and Nora
Stephenson, taken in
1977.

Rev. and Mrs. W.R.
Moore, maternal grand-
parents. Grandpa Moore
was a Nazarene preacher
who had a profound
influence on Jeannie's
life. This photo was
taken in 1954 on their
golden wedding
anniversary.

Jeannie in 1952 at the age of
7; she was in the first grade
in Anson, Texas at the time.

At age 16; already the sultry good
looks of the Harper Valley girl
were evident.

Jeannie, second from the right, as a majorette for Anson High
School's "Tiger Band." Her baton-twirling abilities would become part of her stage show in later years.

Jeannie and Mickey at their "first" wedding
at the First Baptist Church, Anson, Texas.

In 1966 while visiting the taping
of the "Wilburn Brothers Show"
in Nashville just prior to moving
there from Texas. By then, her
compulsion to become a country-
western star had begun.

Bryan Wayne Scott, Jeannie's
nephew, whose death had a
profound influence on her life. At
one point she felt that God had
taken the boy's life because of her
life style in early Nashville years.

Kim Michelle Riley, Jeannie and Mickey's daughter at the age of one. It was the first photo taken of Kim in Tennessee.

A classic photo taken for promotion of "Harper Valley PTA."
Her defiance is complete and her life in a shambles; but
"Harper Valley PTA" is taking off and soaring for the
girl from Anson.

A typical outdoor concert during the Harper Valley days of the early 1970s.

Jeannie and her parents, February 28, 1969, during festivities in honor of Jeannie held by the community of Anson

Jeannie C. Riley and Roy Clark, famed country-western singer and instrumentalist, are presented cowboy hats and keys to the city of Lubbock, Texas, at the annual fair in 1969.

The infamous night when Jeannie's dress was shorn from ankle length to above the knees to conform to her Harper Valley image as she received the "Record of the Year" award presented by the Country Music Association in 1968. From left to right are Johnny Cash, Jeannie, Porter Wagoner, Dolly Parton, Glen Campbell, Bobby Russell and Chet Atkins.

"Live, from the Grand Ole Opry in Nashville, Tennessee" are words familiar to every country-western music fan and especially to a young performer up from Anson, Texas, who has held such a performance dream for much of her life. This was taken during one of Jeannie's many performances at the WSM event.

The three records shown here represent the three million plus
copies that were sold of "Harper Valley PTA" and all are gold.
with Jeannie is Shelby Singleton, president of
Plantation Records.

Jeannie is shown with the late Bing Crosby during a break
in rehearsal for a guest appearance she made in 1968 for
"The Hollywood Palace."

In 1969, with "Harper Valley" riding the top of the charts,
Jeannie appeared on Bob Hope's "Chrysler Special" television
program wearing her familiar turtle-neck sweater.

With the late Elvis Presley in 1969 when both were appearing
in stage shows in Las Vegas.

On a visit home to Anson in 1978, Jeannie and her grand-
mother, Ada Moore, got together for this photo. By then,
her grandfather had died.

This photo of the Rileys was taken in January 1975 after both Jeannie and Mickey had made their new commitments to a much different way of life. Kim is age 10 when this picture was taken.

Photo taken October '80 on the set of the "Johnny Cash
Christmas Special," on which Jeannie guested. She was
spotlighted singing a duet of "Away In A Manger" with Johnny.

Jeannie and songwriter Tom T. Hall, his song,
"Harper Valley PTA" was the spark that ignited her career.

Jeannie was among the celebrities who officially welcomed President Carter to Nashville for his October "Town Hall Meeting" at the Grand Ole Opry House. (October 9, 1980)

11

Bryan's Star

I was upstairs in my big bedroom, snuggled in bed talking to Pete on the phone. Mickey was downstairs watching TV. Suddenly I realized someone was on the phone with us. I gulped, thinking it was Mickey. Then I heard Pete's wife, Ellen, on the extension in their apartment.

"I want to know right now. Do you love my husband?"

I tried to cover. "Of course, I love Pete. He works for me, and I love all my staff."

"That's not what I mean, and you know it." She was almost hissing, her voice was so sharp. "I want to know if you're sleeping with my husband."

"I'm not even sleeping with my own husband," I said truthfully. Mickey, tired of my frigidity, had moved into the guest bedroom across the hall.

"I want to talk to Mickey," Ellen snapped.

"Then talk to him," I said, and quickly hung up. But she didn't call back.

Mickey didn't know how much I cared about Pete, but he knew something was wrong. He started writing sorrowful things. He was not a songwriter, much less a poet. But unable to communicate with me any other way, he began writing. One afternoon I walked into our bedroom. He was sitting in the little office which adjoined the room. He saw me and began shuffling papers. I didn't pay much attention to him, but later, in the same office, I found his unfinished letter to me:

"You just came in a little while ago and saw me writing. I scrambled to get it hidden before you could see it. I guess the thing that hurt the most was you didn't even care enough to wonder who I was writing to . . ."

Stuck under his bed, between the mattress and the springs, I found lyrics to a song he had been working on:

> Little bitty girl like her mother,
> She'll leave and never have a brother,
> I feel like fightin', she's so much like you,
> But I guess being alone is all that I'm due.

"Maybe," he wrote in one poem, "I'll just go back to Texas where somebody loves me."

Mickey was down to skin and bones. He seemed to be living off Jack Daniels whiskey, scarcely eating a thing. One weekend he drove all the way to Memphis to confront me about Pete Terry. He didn't know anything, but he suspected a lot. I was staying in a hotel next to the airport. Mama had called ahead of time and told me Mickey was on the way. Good old Mama; it was the only way she could help. I was alone when Mickey pounded on the door of the hotel room.

I let him in, and he was like a wild man, rushing around the room looking in the closet and under the bed. Finally he calmed down and collapsed into a chair. That was the night I told him the truth about Phil Blackman. It helped ease the tension. I figured if I confessed that much, he'd not ask anything else. I was right.

We stayed up most of the night. I confessed everything about Phil. "I know it sounds like I'm a loose woman," I sobbed, "but I'm not. I just needed somebody to pay me some attention."

"But I'm with you all the time," Mickey moaned.

"But we're alone even when we're together. We stood up in that little church in Anson and said some words, that's all."

"Maybe they were just words to you," Mickey said. "But

I meant it when I said things like 'forever' and 'for better or worse.' "

Mickey looked up me with pleading eyes. "I figured if I worked hard, providing for you and Kim, helping you find your place in the music world—well, that's all I know how to do. I ain't equipped to handle all this. Maybe I should just get out of your life for good."

The battle with Mickey made me face up to the fact that Pete wasn't handling my affairs correctly. Important invitations, like the one to attend the governor's inaugural dinner in Texas, were often left unopened for several weeks. Other inauguration invitations had been discarded. The business was falling behind.

Meanwhile I had hired Ron and Nita Salmon to be my constant conpanions on the road. Ron played guitar in the band, and Nita was my "Girl Friday," fixing my hair, having my clothes ready for changes between shows. They became my "buffer persons"—shielding me from the people who tried to use me. I found myself depending on them more and more as my relationship with Pete deteriorated.

I was virtually living on my bus, the "Harper Valley Express." It was expensive, but I needed it to carry the band and all our equipment. We had bought it in the late spring of 1969 from Kitty Wells. It was an honor to ride down the highway in a bus that had belonged to the "Queen of Country Music." It had gold and black interior in the front "sitting room" with thick, gold carpet. The walls were all tufted, golden vinyl. The rest was sleeping areas. I had a bedroom in the middle with two bunks. I slept on the bottom and Nita had the top. Its decor was turquoise. In the back we had six bunks where Ron and the boys in the band slept. There were also big closets for all our stage clothes. The sound equipment and musical instruments were stored below in the big luggage compartments.

The expenses, however, were astronomical. I was paying the band a full-time salary. Ron and Nita were working full time and were living with us in Nashville, helping with the cooking and with Kim. I was paying Pete a big salary plus expenses, which included a secretary I had to hire for him since he was so far behind. Even though my traveling engagements grossed almost half a million a year, I kept wondering what would happen when the well ran dry, when "Harper Valley PTA" no longer drew the large crowds, and yet the bills went right on.

I discovered later that Mickey had asked Mama to pray for him. He, too, seemed to sense that the problem was spiritual rather than physical or emotional. But like myself, he didn't know where to turn for answers.

It was Mama who warned me, not once but many times, that God had not turned loose of me, and one day all my running around would come to a screeching halt. "You think you're runnin' free, Jeannie," she said. "But you ain't. Like a heifer on a rope, one day you'll take off a'runnin' and almost break your neck, because that rope's tied to God's tree."

It was early August when my sister Helen called frantically from Texas. The doctors were going to have to operate on little Bryan again. Bryan, now five, had seemingly recovered from encephalitis and meningitis four years before. Yet when Helen and Gene had taken him to get his vaccination to register for the first grade, they discovered he had high blood pressure. A blocked artery was causing the problem. During major surgery doctors grafted an artery from his leg into his kidney, but the artery hadn't held. Now they were going to have to operate again. It was extremely serious.

I cancelled all my immediate engagements, and Mickey and I flew home. Mama and Daddy met us at the hospital in Abilene. We arrived the evening before Bryan was to enter surgery. The next morning we were with him when they wheeled him out of the room on his stretcher and down a long hall toward double swinging doors into surgery. I could tell he was frightened. We stood and watched as he disappeared down the hall. But just at the last minute, as Bryan went through the doors, he raised up on the stretcher, looked back at my daddy, and hollered, "Bye, Pa."

Emotions churned inside me as that horrible nightmare of almost five years before kept flickering through my mind. How vivid, how real were those prolonged and agonizing moments of prayer in the ladies room where I knelt with Aunt Ollie and promised God I would give up my dream of a singing career if He would heal Bryan. Back then my sins weren't very deep. So when I repented of wanting to be a country music star, it was easy to give it all up.

But now? How could I knock on His door again? I had been fleeing from Him ever since that time in the ladies room in the hospital in Anson. What must God think about me—Him being so pure and me having done so many wrong things? I tried to pray for Bryan, but I could not get through. The mass of guilt was too thick.

I even went down into the ladies room of the Abilene hospital, wondering if it could bring me close to God as had happened in Anson. But the room was filled with cigarette smoke and smelled of disinfectant. I guessed God didn't hang around restrooms waiting for folks like me to ask Him favors every five years. I stayed only a moment, then fled back down the hall to my family. They all seemed to be as lost as I.

Hours dragged by. The surgery should have been over long before, but there was no word. Night came and the shadows of the outside crept through the windows and surrounded my heart. I looked at Helen. Her eyes reflected the quiet terror in her heart.

The surgeon finally appeared. Bryan was in intensive care. Things seemed good, and they thought he would stabilize. "But," the doctor said, "he still has a long way to go."

About dawn we got a call at Mama's house from Helen who had stayed at the hospital. Bryan's lungs were filling with fluid. They had done a tracheotomy so he could breathe. We rushed back as fast as we could. The pastor from the Baptist church in Anson was there. He shook his head when we walked in.

"The doctors say he's slipping fast. They can't seem to do anything."

I grabbed his hand. "My life is too messed up to pray," I said. "But won't you pray for him?"

He prayed. I don't remember what was said. All I remember was while he was praying I was thinking, *Don't pray that way. Pray for him to be healed. God can heal. I know he can.*

I turned away to look out the window when I heard

someone come through the door of the waiting area. It was the surgeon. He was shaking his head.

None of us was able to cope with it. I broke and ran down the hall. How could Helen and Gene stand it? All I could think was: *It's my fault. I made God a promise. I've broken the promise. Now He's come to punish me.* I thought God was a policeman and if we broke the law, He punished us. Because of my messed up life, Bryan was dead.

Bryan died on Tuesday. He would have been six years old on Wednesday. We buried him on Thursday. In my shocked state I remember Mickey putting his arm around Gene and saying, "Now you folks got enough to worry about without having to think about money. Whatever the insurance doesn't pay, we'll take care of it. We can afford it, and we want to help."

I thought, *That's just like Mickey. Always stepping in to help. There ain't many men like that around.*

Gene put his arms around Mickey and hugged him. "You're the best brother-in-law anybody could ever have." Then he looked over at me. "Don't you ever let this man get away," he said through his tears. "You'd never find another like him—not in a million years."

"I know that," I said, hugging Mickey's arm and wiping my tears on the sleeve of his blue denim work shirt.

After the funeral we went back to Mama and Daddy's to eat lunch. Bryan had looked so pretty in his small casket. We all took turns at the funeral home making sure his little bangs were in place before they closed the casket. But the dread emptiness and the lack of hope were almost more than I could stand.

After lunch I went out into the yard. What good was all the fame? What did it mean that nearly everyone in America knew my name—that I was some kind of Nashville goddess? I couldn't bring him back from the dead. The preacher said he was "with the Lord," but how could I know? I had heard Grandpa Moore preach about heaven and knew he believed in it. Mama, even though she never talked much about it, had caught enough of it from her daddy to believe in it. Helen seemed to believe in it. I wanted to. I wanted so hard to believe little Bryan was in heaven—waiting for the rest of us. But here I was with a lavender Cadillac, money to fly around the world, three closets jammed full of clothes. I had boots I hadn't even worn. Gold records. Pictures of me and the president. Thinking about the peace of heaven made it all seem so empty.

I looked at my folks' modest, little frame house, painted a soft green. It was surrounded by a big yard. The vegetable garden in back was at its peak. They had struggled all their lives, and this is what they had to show for it. Little Bryan had lived only six years. And all he had now was a mound of dirt out there in the cemetery. Is this all there is to life?

I got in Daddy's yellow and black '56 Chevy and backed out onto the street. The cemetery was about a mile outside the city limits, on Highway 180 going east toward Fort Worth. It was a hot August afternoon. The car didn't have an air conditioner. The hot, West Texas wind blew through my hair and dried my tears against my face. I didn't know whether I could take any more. I felt responsible for Bryan's death. I needed something, some kind of sign, to let me know everything was not lost.

There was a little dirt road into the cemetery. I pulled up beside the fresh mound of dirt covered with flowers left over from the funeral. There was a small, gray, metal marker at the end of the grave, a temporary marker until they could set in place the marble slab with the little rabbit on top: *Bryan Wayne Scott*. We had called him "Bryan Rabbit" or "Bunny Rabbit." I knelt beside the grave, the tears flowing.

God, I know I'm not worthy to ask You for anything. I'm not even sure You're there. And if You are, why would You mess with someone like me who's let You down so many times? But You've got to be there.

My spirit told me I was not alone even though there was no one else in the cemetery. The sky was clear. The hot wind blew up little puffs of dust. In the field next to the cemetery tumbleweeds were being rolled north toward the panhandle by a south wind. The sun was over my right shoulder. At 3:45 p.m. it was still high in the big, empty

Texas sky. Yet someone was there. I could feel it.

The memories were now so real. There was Grandpa Moore. As kids we had been ashamed of his street preaching. Ashamed of his hell fire and damnation. Ashamed of his tears as he called people to commit their lives to Jesus Christ. Ashamed because some of the people in Anson made fun of him.

They called him "Mad Dog Moore" because when he talked about the grace of God he would begin to cry, his nose running as he wept, specks of saliva coming from his mouth. One man had once spit in his face on the street corner—an ugly stream of tobacco juice. Grandpa had turned the other cheek and said, "God bless you, brother."

I remembered how he loved to preach about heaven. He loved to tell the story, over and over, of the angels at the empty tomb saying, "He is not here, He is risen." But Bryan was not risen. He was under that pile of dirt, the casket lid closed on his little face, his dark bangs so still across his white forehead.

Grandpa Moore's story of the girl in the cemetery flashed through my mind. *She was a girl like me,* I thought, *that Mary Magdalene who came to the grave of her loved One. She wasn't worthy either. She was even worse than me—a prostitute, a woman of the streets who had become one of His followers.* She came as I had come to Bryan's grave, weeping, grieving. Then she heard a voice behind her in the early morning darkness calling her name.

"Mary! Mary!"

"It's the sweetest sound this side of heaven," Grandpa Moore had said, the tears running down his face as he stood behind that rickety, old wooden pulpit preaching to the handful of country folks in his little one-room church building. "Nothing's so sweet as hearing the Savior call your name in the darkness."

"Oh, God," I wailed, looking up into the sky. "God, I need You to call my name. If You're there? If You see me down here? Please listen? I've got to know there's more to life than this earth. I've got to know Bryan is not lost forever, that this is not the end, that I will see him again. Let me know that there is a chance for me, too. I'll try to make things right, God. Please, oh, please, give me some kind of a sign."

I didn't know what I was asking for. Grandpa Moore was plowing in the cotton fields when the Lord gave him a sign. For months he had been "under conviction," believing the Lord had some kind of call on his life. That morning, plowing in the field behind a mule, holding onto the plow handle, he cried out to God.

Instantly he was struck blind. Grandma Ada and the children were all out there in the field when it happened. They saw the crusts form on his eyes as he dropped to his knees beside the plowed furrow. Like the Apostle Paul on the road to Damascus, he had been touched by the mighty hand of God. He had to crawl out of the field on his hands and knees, the big dirt clods clinging to the knees of his overalls. Leaving the old mule behind for Grandma and the kids to bring to the house, he had made it across the field and finally spread himself out on the ground before God. It wasn't until he answered the call to preach, almost an hour later, that his sight returned and the scales on his eyes disappeared.

At that time he told God he would preach until his voice was gone and his legs failed. "I'll preach Your word as long as my legs will carry me, Lord. If they fail, I'll preach on my knees, crawling like I did in that cotton field."

I actually saw it come to that. He had finally built his little one-room church, but he was old and weak by then. His teeth were gone and his eyes dim. One Sunday his legs collapsed under him. He dropped to his knees by the pulpit but never stopped preaching, his voice still strong as he fulfilled his promise to the Lord.

Deep inside I wanted something like that to happen to me. In fact, I yearned for it. I felt so dirty, so unclean. Like a child who had misbehaved, I wanted discipline—but I was afraid of it at the same time. Somehow the idea of being struck blind because you're running from God seemed right. Deep inside I knew my life was displeasing to God, and I deserved punishment. Perhaps this was the time it would come.

Maybe, like Grandpa, I would be struck blind in the

cemetery and have to crawl all the way home, scratched and bleeding, and give my heart to the Lord. Maybe He wanted me to give up singing and become a missionary. Maybe He wanted me to start singing for Him, traveling around the country and giving my testimony of how God had struck me blind in the cemetery and then raised me up in purity. I could almost picture myself at some altar in a church, weeping and crying, confessing all my sins to God. But first I needed to be struck blind.

I didn't know what to expect, kneeling there by the grave, looking south toward Abilene. I had heard Grandpa Moore's story a dozen times, but that was for him. Why would God be so kind as to strike me blind? Only the father who loves his children spanks them. It was hard to believe God could love a person like me.

The sun was blistering hot. Not yet 4 p.m., it would be several hours before it dropped low enough to pick up the shadows of the leafless mesquite bushes and the squatty junipers, their green contrasting against the dusty brown earth of the cemetery. The tears had stopped, drying almost immediately in the still dry air. The wind had stopped blowing. The big windmill in a nearby field stood motionless. Heat waves rose in vertical ripples from the plowed cotton fields, forming water mirages on the horizon. There was no sound. Even my heart was at ease as I leaned back on my heels, kneeling beside the freshly dug dirt. It was as if the whole world, for that moment, had stopped.

Suddenly, in the southern sky, a sparkle of light appeared. It was like the reflection of the sun off a piece of bright metal. Tiny in the sky. Sparkling. But it wasn't a reflection from an airplane. It was a different color from the sun. It grew bigger and brighter, like a giant star moving toward me at an incredible rate of speed, growing in intensity and brightness, sparkling white like a diamond. Gradually it stopped moving and hung in the sky over Abilene.

"What is it?" I asked aloud, awed but not frightened.

"It's a star," a quiet voice said in my spirit.

"In the middle of the day?" I asked again, out loud. "Why a star?"

"You asked about Bryan. I'm showing you My new star

in heaven."

It seemed so natural, kneeling there, talking to God. I was not afraid as I thought I would be. In fact, I didn't even think about it at the time. I heard no voice, but the words in my heart, deep in my understanding, were as vivid as if they had been spoken aloud. Only I was speaking, answering Him back as though He were an old friend who had walked beside me all my life. We chatted for a few moments about the star—and Bryan. He answered every question I asked but kept coming back in a matter-of-fact way, saying I had asked and He was answering.

In that instant I knew. High above the dusty cemetery. High above the mesquite bushes. High above Texas. Bryan was with Jesus. The star began to fade, to withdraw into the southern sky like a small dot. I wanted to reach out. To hold. To pull it back.

"Oh, hello, Bryan!" I shouted.

Instantly the star reappeared, rushing back toward me until it dazzled me with its brightness. It hung there for a second. Then it vanished.

Suddenly the wind was blowing, a big tumbleweed bouncing across the open cemetery. I felt my hair brushing against my face, and the world was once again in motion on its axis.

"I don't know how I'm going to do it," I said, standing to my feet. "But I'm gonna see you again, little Bunny Rabbit."

I was not talking down toward the grave, I realized. My face was still lifted toward the sky where the star had been. Something had happened to me. It was different from that experience in the ladies room of the hospital in Anson. This time God didn't seem to be requiring anything. Maybe He hadn't required anything then either, but I had tried to give it to Him just the same. But this time God didn't seem to want any kind of promise. I guess He knew I couldn't keep it anyway. He didn't even seem to be demanding that I repent or change or anything. I knew, had He wanted, He could have struck me blind. But He hadn't. All He had done was reveal Himself to me. And He was so much different from the way I had Him pictured in my mind. This time He was a God of great and infinite love and mercy. He hadn't taken Bryan to punish me. He just wasn't that kind of God. I didn't know why He had taken Bryan. That was His business. But for whatever reason it was, I could trust Him. I didn't know what He was going to do with my life, either. I wasn't even worried about it anymore. Somehow, though, I sensed He was in control of things and in the end—what was that Mama once said to me? "And we know that all things work together for good to them that love God."

As I left the cemetery, I realized for the first time the meaning of the sign at the gate: Mt. Hope Cemetery. I smiled as I pulled the car out onto the narrow road and headed back toward the little green house.

"Thank You," I whispered.

To my left was the old, rusty, barbed-wire fence with six strands of sagging wire. A lonely farmhouse stood in the middle of the plowed field. It was the same Texas I had always known, but something was different. Maybe it was me.

"Thank You," I whispered again into the dirty windshield of Daddy's old car. "This time I'll not make You any promises. But You haven't seen the last of me."

12

The Dark Pit

espite the vision in the cemetery and what I knew was a direct word from God, I did not change my life style. And I continued with my astrology. Like a lot of entertainers, I thought it was chic. Astrology was one of the ways I chose to find direction for my life. My bookshelves were filled with occult books on astrology and the signs of the zodiac. I discovered, for instance, that Pete Terry was a Gemini—and that Geminis have two faces. That explained, I thought, why I could be so enchanted with him and so turned off at the same time.

On the other hand, I was a Libra. Libras, I read in one book, are more honest than Geminis. Another book said Libras, while being honest, can also be deceptive. I identified with both extremes.

Pete and I spent a lot of time discussing the subject.

"If you were anything but a Gemini," I told him, "I could really dig you."

"No problem," he laughed. "I'll change the date I was born."

But there didn't seem to be much hope that Pete could be born again. Nor that I would either.

In fact, Pete didn't seem to think I needed a rebirth. "You know, deep inside, you're not the Harper Valley girl," he said. "Folks see you that way, and I am forced to promote you that way. But those boots and miniskirts are not natural for you. The more I'm around you, the more I see through all that sassy stuff. In fact, I think you're probably a lot more religious than you let folks know."

I needed to hear that. I wanted to hear that. I found myself drawn to Pete as a close friend who seemed to understand, who loved to listen to my endless questions.

The band, however, was concerned. They knew Mickey was not entirely out of my life. Several of them talked to me about it. They felt bad for Mickey because they respected him, but more urgent was their fear that Mickey might become violent when he discovered how close I was to Pete. After all, as one of the musicians said candidly, how much can one man take?

The thing finally blew up on a tour of Texas. My bus driver leaked the word to Mickey that I was spending too much time with Pete. We were in Dallas when Ron Salmon, my guitarist, pulled me aside.

"Mickey called me this afternoon," he said. "He's mad as a hornet about you and Pete."

I was scared. Deep down I wanted things out in the open. But I dreaded what would happen.

"Mickey said the whole family had a powwow last night," Ron continued. "Your mom and dad were there, and so were Helen and Gene."

I felt the color draining from my face. "They're plotting to get me," I stammered.

"I don't think they are after you as much as they're after Pete," he said.

"Well, at least we've got a few days to work things out," I said. "We're supposed to fly to California tomorrow for a special and won't get home until the weekend. Maybe things will cool off by then."

"I don't think so," Ron said seriously. "I think you ought to be frightened. Mickey's mad enough to kill."

I thought of that scene in the Memphis hotel room when Mickey had almost broken down the door. He was really after Pete that night, and I had stalled him by telling him about Phil Blackman. But as for now, we all needed to

The Dark Pit'

119

catch the plane for Los Angeles.

The California trip centered on an appearance with Oral Roberts for a new nationwide television series to promote his university in Tulsa. I was to be the guest artist for the first show.

I didn't realize at the time how risky it was for Oral Roberts to invite the girl who epitomized a generation in rebellion as his first guest. Nor did I realize that this appearance would be a turning point in my life.

I felt awkward during the rehearsal for the Oral Roberts special. As always I wore my miniskirt with a blouse that showed several inches of cleavage, but for the first time I felt "undressed." Glancing around I realized I was the only one so scantily attired. Would I get Oral Roberts in trouble with his audience? I discovered later that he invited non-religious artists like me to appear for two reasons. First, through them he wanted to reach today's generation. Second, he hoped these artists would have an experience on the program that would make them seek God.

During rehearsal I went back to my dressing room and changed my costume. The two songs I chose were: "There Never Was a Time We Didn't Love" and "Country Girl." Both were clean. The taping was uneventful, and afterwards I hurried back to the dressing room to change clothes so I could catch the plane back to Amarillo, Texas, and rejoin our bus tour.

Oral and Evelyn Roberts followed me to the dressing room where they pulled up chairs and sat down. I was fidgety, knowing I had only a few minutes to catch the plane. But I didn't want to be impolite, so I tried to relax as they complimented us on our performance. Then they talked about other Nashville singers, especially Connie Smith who had become a Christian just a few years before. I had developed a deep respect for Connie; I knew she had something I didn't have, but I was reluctant to find out what it was, afraid I might have to give up some of the things I had my heart set on.

"Jeannie," Oral said, looking at me intently, "I believe that you are in a great transition period. One day you will come back to your roots and will be singing for the Lord."

Flustered, I shook my head and said, "Brother Roberts, I'd really like to be a Christian, but my life's too messed up."

"If you want to make a start in this direction, Evelyn and I want to help," he replied. "For one thing, we want to pray for you. Not just tonight, but in the days to come we'll be praying. Also, I'd like to lead you in a prayer which will be the first step in your journey back to God. Would you be willing to repeat this short prayer after me?"

"If it'll help with this mess I'm in right now," I said, "I sure will."

"God knows all about the mess you're in," Oral said, taking my hand. I repeated after him what he called "the sinner's prayer." "Dear Lord, I confess I'm a sinner. I can't do anything to save myself. But I believe You love me and You sent Your Son, Jesus Christ, to pay the penalty of my sin. I repent of my sins, Lord, and I accept Jesus Christ as my Savior. I pray You will send Your Holy Spirit to me so He can also become the Lord of my life."

The prayer was over, and I realized I had missed my plane. The Robertses didn't know they'd made me late—and even if they had, what they were doing somehow seemed more important than anything else. Evelyn reached out and took my hand once again. "God has something great for you," she said. "You may have to go through the dark valley before you see His full light, but He will walk with you every step of the way."

They were gone, and I stood looking at myself in the mirror. Where had I put my suitcase? Where was that other clothing bag? Where could I charter a plane to get to Amarillo on time? What if Mickey was there waiting for me? There was no time to remember the prayer. The problems of my world had to be dealt with.

The private plane got us to Amarillo just moments before the show started. I dressed on the way to the concert hall, combing my hair in the car and finishing my make-up backstage while the boys were setting up the equipment. We were on stage less than 45 minutes after we landed.

Mama had flown out from Nashville to visit in Texas and was going to ride back with us. My bus driver had already given her an earful about my conduct. Mickey was still at home, waiting. The pressure of the tight schedule, knowing Mama was in the audience, knowing we were fixing to leave for home that night and I'd have to face my family the next day were almost more than I could take.

Standing in the wings that night, just before the show began, I prayed the first prayer I'd ever prayed before going on stage: "I don't deserve to be helped, Lord, but please help me anyway." I guess enough of Oral Roberts' prayer had penetrated to get me through Amarillo. After that, I suspected, I would be on my own again.

I'll never forget the wild scene on the bus as we rolled out of Amarillo into the Texas night and headed toward Nashville. It started with Mama talking to me about right and wrong, what I was doing to little Kim and my wrong relationship with Pete Terry. I was tired and angry and told her I didn't want to talk about it.

All of a sudden she exploded. It was the old anger I hadn't seen since she blew up once at Daddy for drinking. "I can't face this," she screamed. "You're hurting everyone around you who loves you. You've just gone crazy over men."

"Well, Mickey's no angel," I shouted back. "He's going with that girl who works for Shelby. I even heard he loaned her money to pay her rent. He may be 'waiting' for me, but he sure ain't waiting alone."

Just saying it out loud in front of everyone on the bus somehow justified what I was doing. Maybe his wrongs made mine less serious.

Mama wouldn't hear. I tried to calm her down, but there was no way. She was screaming at the top of her voice about Pete while Ron and Nita and the others listened in embarrassment.

"Mama, you don't know what you're talking about. Pete and I are just good friends, that's all."

"That's a lie," she retorted. "I don't believe anything you say anymore."

I finally got her back into her seat, but then she jumped up again, not making much sense, just demanding that I stop seeing Pete. That made me angry. The more she carried on, the uglier I reacted. She had a way of just telling me what to do and what not to do without giving me any reasons.

"I don't understand it," she cried. "You get rid of one fellow and then latch onto that small time deejay. You've flown all the way around the world and landed on a turd."

"It's not right for you to talk that way about him," I hollered.

"Well, he's got no right breaking up a family."

"Mama, you might as well face it. This family's already broken up. It was broken up long before I met Pete. Mickey just isn't the man for me."

As we rode across Arkansas and Tennessee, it was like taking a bus ride through hell. As we pulled into Nashville, I knew I was going to have to tell Mickey the truth and end both the personal and business relationship with Pete Terry.

Mickey and I talked for two days after I got home. We sat in my room and cried together. We agreed that we had drifted too far apart to ever come back together.

"I knew it," Mickey agonized. "I knew it all the time. God, it hurts, but we've got to get it out in the open where we can see it."

Mama and Daddy were downstairs and heard Mickey banging his fist on the wall. Before I knew it they were in the room. It was the first time Daddy had intervened in my life.

"That gal right there," he said, pointing to Mama, "is the only woman in my life. I married her more'n 30 years ago, and there ain't been no other woman—and there won't be till I die. That's the way it's supposed to be."

"Daddy, you just don't understand me," I was crying. "All I want is for you and Mama to love me and realize I love you. This is not personal stuff against you all."

"You don't love us, girl," Daddy replied. "You don't even know what love is. Love is something you do. If you loved us, you wouldn't be doing stuff like this."

"This has nothing to do with y'all," I cried. "I do love you. You don't understand. All I want you to do is be a daddy and a mama to me, and let me work out my life for myself."

"Young 'un," he said, his voice stern and his eyes narrowed, "we didn't raise you like this. I may not a'been much of a daddy to you, but I taught you better'n this. Some things is sacred—and marriage is one of them. You don't just walk away from a man just because he don't thrill you anymore. Love is hard stuff, girl. It's earning a living and supporting a family. It's raising children to know the difference between right and wrong. It's something you do whether you feel like it or not. Love ain't like the flu. It ain't something you catch, and something you get over. It's saying something with your mouth that you intend to back up with your life. That's what love is, and you don't know nothing about that."

I was crying so hard I couldn't see. Daddy had never talked to me like that. I knew in my heart he was right, but there wasn't anything I could do about it. Mickey came to my rescue.

"Folks, I think you all just oughta leave now. Jeannie and me'll work out our own problems. Trouble is, there's too many people giving advice, butting into our lives and telling us what to do. I think we might be able to work things out if everybody would just leave us alone."

"You're making a sad mistake, son," Daddy said. "Nora and me are on your side. But if that's what you want, we'll go."

Daddy and Mama took Mickey literally—even though he didn't mean it that way. They left the room and began to pack to go back to Texas. It was as if the whole world was coming to an end.

The next day I confronted Pete. He knew it was coming. I was sad about it, but I had no choice. The personal relationship had already deteriorated and all that was left were the business matters. He still had two years to go on his contract, but I went ahead and asked Gene Scott, my sister Helen's husband, to leave his job at the bank in Anson and come to Nashville to help with my business affairs. I told Pete just to stay in his office and draw his salary. As far as I was concerned, everything else was ended.

The next months were like a bad dream. I read my horoscope daily, growing more depressed all the time. I was living on my bus for weeks on end as the cities blended into one: Memphis, Jonesboro, Wichita Falls, Pecos, San Diego, Twin Rivers, Tacoma, then a flying trip to Philadelphia with side engagements in Trenton, York and Scranton. The highway was my home. I had no family but that endless sea of faces, whistling and shouting.

I wrote a song, "Mama, Does Your Little Girl Sound Sad?" It reflected my mood at the time.

> Hello, Mama, I just called to say good-night.
> I just had to know if you and Pa were all right.
> I sound hoarse?
> Oh well, of course, I sing a lot,
> But they're just words—there's not a song left in my heart.

The chorus went:

> Oh, oh, Mama, does your little girl sound sad?
> I'm sorry if I've made you all feel bad,
> But it just gets lonesome out here on the road
> With a heart packed full of memories
> And a suitcase for a home.

Mama and Daddy had left. Pete was out of the picture. With everything falling apart it didn't make any sense to try to hold onto Mickey, either. If I was to ever find happiness, I'd have to do it my way. Alone.

13

Riley vs. Riley

I asked Mickey for the divorce on Thanksgiving night 1970 while we were driving home from friends. Mickey was at the wheel of the fancy Cadillac with the black vinyl top. Kim was in the back seat asleep.

"There's no use pretending any longer," I told him. "I've messed up my own life and am dragging everybody down with me."

"You keep saying that," Mickey said, staring ahead at the road. "But that's just because you keep forgetting what it was like in the beginning. You know, sometimes it's as important to look back as to look ahead."

"Mickey, why don't we just admit it's all over? You keep hanging on, saying we'll make it somehow. But we won't. It's been over for a long time. I've made up my mind. I want a divorce. The quicker the better."

He slowed for traffic and then made a left turn onto a tree-lined street that was a shortcut to our house. He was expressionless, but his cheeks were wet with tears.

"I know it hurts," I said. "It hurts me, too. But we've been hurtin' each other too long. And think of little Kim back there. She's almost five years old now. It's not right for her to grow up on a battleground. At least it will give her some peace."

"Whatever you want, that's it," he said. "I won't give you no trouble."

We pulled up in the driveway, and he cut the engine. He sat for a long time, staring at the dark house, his hands still on the steering wheel. "You'll come back some day. I know you will."

"Mickey, don't say that. You're just hanging onto something that isn't real."

He opened the door, and I felt the cold air from the outside rush against my face. "You'll come back," he said with a soft finality. "And I'll be waiting. I'm not going anywhere. It's you that's on the run."

The next morning I woke and went into the guest room where Mickey was sleeping. He had already gotten up but was just sitting on the edge of the bed, staring at the wall.

"You changed your mind?" he asked.

"No," I answered simply, standing in the door and thinking how pathetic he looked.

"Then let's get a lawyer today and get it over with."

We sat down with an attorney that afternoon. It was a wild conversation with both of us trying to take the blame.

"No, it's not her fault," Mickey argued. "I've failed, too. It takes two to mess up, don't it?"

"That's not true," I said. "He doesn't want the divorce. I do. It's my fault."

The attorney sat behind his desk listening and finally said, "If you two can't come up with something else, I'm going to send you home. You can't get a divorce just because you want to. There has to be some reason."

We finally settled on "mental cruelty." I knew I was signing my name to a lie. It was strictly selfishness, but that wasn't a good enough reason for the courts.

When it came to the property settlement, Mickey said, "I came into this relationship with the shirt on my back—and nothing else. I'm gonna go out the same way."

"No," I sobbed. "That's not right. Our assets are as much yours as mine."

Mickey just shook his head. Turning to the lawyer he said, "It's her money. She's made it on her singing. All I want is about $500 to get me back to Texas for a few weeks. I'll borrow one of the cars until I can get going again. That's all I want. Everything else belongs to her."

The decision was final. Mickey wasn't going to back down.

Then he got up from the table where we were sitting and walked to the window. I knew what was going through his mind. I could see his shoulders sag as he thought of little Kim. He loved her so. It stabbed me. I loved her too, but someone else always did the important things with her—bathing her, washing her clothes, fixing her hair, feeding her, reading her books. It seemed that all I did was breeze through her room between trips, pick her up, cuddle her, tell her I loved her, then hand her back to my sister or my mother or whoever else was taking care of her and rush off to the next engagement.

Mickey always took time for Kim. Even in the midst of our worst periods, he would come in from work, tired and worn out, and go straight to her. I might be in the kitchen cooking supper with Mama or sitting at my desk talking to some agent on the phone, but Mickey would always go straight for Kim. He'd take her outside and play with her, help her ride her tricycle. I knew all that was running through his mind as he stood at the window looking at the sky.

His voice broke as he tried to speak. "It's not right to take Kim away from her mother. She's so much like her mama and little girls need . . ." He wasn't able to finish.

He left that evening. He said he couldn't spend another night in the house with me. He wanted to take Kim with him the first night just to keep from being all alone in the motel room. I consented and told him he could call me the next morning, and I'd come after her.

He had chosen a run-down hotel, the kind lonely people would pick. When I got there he was sitting on a saggy old bed in a room with wallpaper peeling and the plaster in the bathroom dark and mildewed. I thought of Elvis Presley's "Heartbreak Hotel" and could hardly see through my tears as I put Kim in the car. He stood there in the door of his room, hand raised, waving at his little girl as she leaned over the back seat and waved through the back window, shouting, "'Bye, Daddy. Have a good time. Be careful. I love you. 'Bye, Daddy, bye-bye from Kim."

Mickey gave me a letter which I still have tucked in my Bible. In it he wrote how God was taking those things away from him which he had put ahead of the Lord. He guessed West Texas would always be his home . . . how much like me Kim was . . . how he wanted me to raise her to be good . . . that he would love me till the day he died.

The night before I left for an appearance in New Mexico, Mickey came back by the house. He had been drinking. Not much. But just enough to keep from being emotional.

"Jeannie, I feel sorry for you," he said. "You've shut the door to all those who really love you. You've closed the door on me, your Mama and Daddy, even to Helen and Gene. The only ones you listen to now are those who care for you because of who you are today—and for what you have. Someday it's gonna come home to you mighty hard, and you're gonna be sorry."

It was the excuse I had been looking for to get angry, to ease my guilt because he was such a nice guy.

"I don't have to take that from you," I said. "You were the one who told my folks to get out of the house, not me."

"I didn't want them to leave. I just wanted you to come to your senses. But it didn't do any good. You've gone ahead with the divorce. I'm going along with it, but it wouldn't be right if I didn't speak truth to you. You're making the biggest mistake of your life, and one day you'll regret it."

"I don't want to hear this."

"I know it's hard to hear," Mickey said calmly. "But it's going to be a lot harder if you keep this up."

I grabbed a tiny figurine off my dresser and threw it in his direction. It didn't come close. It smashed against the wall and fell in slivers to the floor. "Nobody understands! I've just got to find myself!"

I ran toward him, my fists flailing. He grabbed me by the shoulders and held me off. I broke free and flew out the door of the bedroom and down the stairs. Halfway down I began to trip and fall, ending up in a crouching position against the front door at the bottom of the stairs, screaming. Mickey was right behind me, trying to pull

me to my feet. From some place in the other room little
Kim had appeared. She was standing near the door, her
own little terrified voice joining in the cacophony of wails
and shouts.

Mickey pulled me up on my feet and slapped my face.
"Look at you," he shouted. "Look how selfish you are.
There's your little girl standing there frightened to death at
the way you're acting, and you keep on screaming. This is
what I've been talking about. You don't care about nobody
but yourself. You don't care about me, about your folks, not
even about your little girl. All you want is someone to feel
sorry for you. And if you can't get it from me, you'll get
it someplace. There'll always be some man around who'll
give you just what you want if you make enough noise."

Stunned, I looked down at little Kim, her hair hanging
stringy around her face, white with terror. Her little brown
freckles were almost bleached out with fear. I looked at
Mickey's strong face, his eyes burning into me.

"I love you," he said. "But I can't live with you the way
you are. No one can live with you. You can't even live with
yourself."

His hands dropped from my shoulders, and he stood there
looking at me. Exhausted from the strain which had just
swept through me, I reached out and started to lean against
his shoulder. He pushed me back, snorted and wheeled
through the door. He was gone. I stood there staring at
Kim. Her eyes were round.

"You love me, Mama?" she whimpered.

I fell on my knees and reached out for her. She came
timidly, afraid I might explode again. "Oh yes, little darlin',
Mama loves you."

"You love Daddy, Mama?"

I held her tightly, crying softly. I could not answer.

I still do not understand how in the midst of this desert
of thorns and scorpions there were little bushes that kept
burning. In the midst of what was the darkest time of my
life, there were little glimpses of light. For example, a newspaper interview.

A columnist, LaWayne Satterfield, who wrote for the Music

City News, had called and asked to see me. For some reason, I not only granted the interview, but I agreed to go to LaWayne's apartment rather than insisting she come to my office. Since I had to make a trip to Kinda-Mama's with Kim, I told the columnist I would stop by her place since it was on the way. But I never got to Kinda-Mama's that night.

During the interview, LaWayne asked me about Mickey. I've seldom been able to hide anything from anyone, and before I realized it I was telling her about the tremendous void in my life, the deep sense of being empty and unfulfilled. I told her that I felt God had something for me to do, and I couldn't find what it was—I didn't know how to respond.

She reached over on the little table next to her chair and picked up a Bible and began to read to me. The words were so familiar, yet so far away:

Let not your heart be troubled: ye believe in God, believe also in Me. In My Father's house are many mansions: if it were not so, I would have told you. I go to prepare a place for you (John 14:1-2).

I felt something happen to me as she read. The turmoil and soul-wrenching of the day before were gone. There was peace. I closed my eyes and rested.

. . . I am the way, the truth, and the life: no man cometh unto the Father, but by Me . . . And whatsoever ye shall ask in My name, that will I do, that the Father may be glorified in the Son. If you shall ask anything in My name, I will do it . . . I will not leave you comfortless: I will come to you . . . Peace I leave with you, My peace I give unto you: not as the world giveth, give I unto you . . . (John 14).

She read the entire 14th chapter of the gospel of John. I looked over at Kim. She was asleep on the couch. LaWayne told me how much Jesus Christ meant to her, how He had helped her through her own tough times, and how she knew He wanted to help me. She suggested that the vacuum in my heart could only be filled with the Spirit of Jesus, that nothing else would ever do—not some man, not being number one in the nation. Only Jesus.

There was a ring of truth in what she was saying, but I knew I wasn't ready yet to make a commitment. At the same time, I knew that living in limbo was probably the most miserable type of life. Better to be sold out to the devil—or sold out to God—than trying to stay in both camps.

I don't remember whether LaWayne ever wrote up the interview or not. I do know that being with her was one of the bright spots in my walk through the darkness.

When I got in the car that night to drive back home, with Kim asleep on the seat beside me, I turned on the radio. I didn't listen at first, still caught up in what had just taken place. It had been years since I had seen anyone with an open Bible and even longer since anyone had read it to me.

Then I heard Ferlin Husky singing on the car radio a song titled, "Open Up the Book and Take a Look." I could hardly believe it! What did all this mean? A newspaper columnist opened up the Bible and read it to me and told me that only Jesus Christ could solve my problems. Then the radio played a song about the Bible.

"You're trying to tell me something, aren't You, God?" I said out loud in the car.

Then, back to back on the radio, without any chatter in between, Lynn Anderson's latest single was playing.

"Forgive her," a little voice inside me whispered. "Love her right now."

Ever since that night at the awards banquet when I appeared on stage in that ridiculous dress, I had felt unforgiveness toward Lynn Anderson. Someone told me later she had made some kind of snide remark about me and the way I looked. I realize now that probably everyone in the auditorium made the same kind of remark. But for some reason, the only one I heard about was Lynn. Now here she was on the radio, singing her latest song, and I just prayed asking God what He was trying to tell me.

"Forgive her and love her."

"But how, Lord?" I asked.

"Just think about what a good singer she is," He seemed to say.

Lynn is a great performer, a real professional. She has

a dynamic voice and knows how to use it to full effect. Beautiful, with long blonde hair, she is easy to love.

The more I thought about her good qualities, the more I appreciated her. And suddenly the forgiveness was there. What a stupid thing to hold something against someone when they might not have even thought it, much less said it. All the unforgiveness had done was to hurt me.

Two weeks later I was playing a night club in Sacramento, California. We were staying at the Holiday Inn, and before leaving for the performance Ron and Nita went with me to the motel restaurant for a bite to eat. I had just finished loading my plate at the salad bar when I looked up and saw Connie Smith come into the room. She spotted me and came directly to our table. She introduced us to Coleman McDuff, the Pentecostal preacher who was with her and in whose church she was singing. She was glowing, sparkling and carrying the biggest Bible I had ever seen.

I felt awkward in her presence. Connie wasn't trying to be number one anymore. She was content with her life, content to go around the country and sing in churches. She was obviously unembarrassed to be in the presence of a Pentecostal preacher and carrying her own Bible out in public. We chatted for a few minutes, Connie doing most of the talking about the Lord, about her relationship with Him, how happy she was.

Then it was time to go, and we headed out to the bus to drive to the night club where I was to perform. Ron Salmon was deep in thought as we sat down together.

"You know, I come from a Pentecostal background," he said.

"Well, don't all of us have some kind of Christian background?"

"Yes, but just having a background ain't enough, is it?" he said, almost to himself. Then he added, "Connie seemed so alive, so real. She's not like the rest of us with our masks on stage and our misery the rest of the time. She was just as happy and real back there as she is on stage."

"She doesn't sing the clubs anymore," I said. "She doesn't have a band traveling with her anymore. She's taken a big step down to sing for God."

"What do you think about that?" Ron asked.

"I admire her," I said. "I think I admire her more than any other woman I know."

"But she probably won't ever be number one again."

"Is that everything?" I asked.

My sister Helen knew about my plans for divorce, but I asked her to keep it a secret until I got back from a trip I was making to Germany in December. I planned to go to Texas for Christmas. Mickey's folks would be there, and I didn't want them to know until after Christmas.

Helen came by before I left for Germany and took me out to lunch. When we got back to the house, we sat in the car talking.

"Jeannie, why don't you just pray for God to give you the answers?"

"I don't want to pray," I said. "Besides, I know what the answer will be."

"What do you mean?"

"The Bible says that divorce is wrong. So why pray when you know what the answer is going to be ahead of time?"

"You know the Lord wants the best things for His children," Helen said. "He doesn't want you to be unhappy. He wants you to be fulfilled. Have you ever thought about praying for His will to become your will? Then you'll be doing what you want, and it'll be what He wants, too."

It sounded like a batch of words to me. "Look, Helen," I asked, "why doesn't everyone just leave me alone and let me do it my way? Why should my problems with Mickey get everyone so upset? Can't you love me the way I am?"

"You don't understand, Jeannie," Helen said, taking my hand. "We do love you. And because we love you, when you're unhappy, we're unhappy, too. That's the way it is in the family—especially the family of God."

"Then there's no reason for you to be upset," I said. "One day I'm going to find my happiness."

Helen looked at me for long seconds, then she said softly, "Will you? Really?"

I felt the tears coming and, rather than let her see them, I pulled away and opened the car door to get out. "You just don't understand," I said. "Nobody does."

That afternoon Helen gave me two books. One was a book by Pat Boone, *A New Song*. "It's different," Helen said. "But since it happened to Pat Boone, I thought you'd want to read it."

The other book she gave me was a copy of *The Living Bible*. "Instead of all those astrology books," she said, "why not read the Word of God? I want you to promise me you'll read the book of John. Just do it for me, will you?"

I promised, but even though this was the second time the book of John had been mentioned, I wasn't sure I would do it. I suspected that in the pages of that book was the power to change my life.

Early the next morning, Saturday, I called Connie Smith. I had known for a long time if things ever got bad enough I'd turn to Connie. There was something in her life that rang true. I didn't understand all she had been through. She had divorced her first husband and married another man. At the time that happened I was shocked. Then Connie had become a Christian and did something else I didn't understand. She divorced her second husband saying she had taken him away from his family. Then she remarried a respected Christian man. I didn't understand all that, but somehow I knew there was something real in Connie Smith. I had always admired her from afar, and we had occasionally been on shows together. But this time I needed more than a friendly hello. I needed help.

"Jeannie, I can't tell you what to do about Mickey," Connie said softly. "But I can't see any good coming from a mother being away from her child."

"But what can I do? It seems I belong to everyone but me."

Her voice was quiet as she answered, quoting from Psalm 100. "Know ye that the Lord He is God: it is He that hath made us, and not we ourselves: we are His people, and the sheep of His pasture." She paused, then continued. "Jeannie, you don't belong to anyone but God." Then she asked, "How about going to church with me tomorrow?"

I met her Sunday evening in front of her church. The pastor was the son of a famous country singer. I knew some of the Nashville stars, including Johnny Cash, attended the church on occasion. Even so, I felt self-conscious. It had been a long time since I was in church. Yet standing there in a churchy dress, waiting for Connie, I watched as the nippy autumn wind picked up the few remaining brown leaves on the lawn and blew them down the sidewalk. I felt good. Clean.

At the close of the service the pastor gave what I realized was a standard altar call. It started by asking everyone who had a need to raise his hand. Then, if you had raised your hand, he asked you to stand. Then he asked all those standing to come forward and kneel at the altar for prayer. If anyone had a need, I did. I raised my hand. I stood. And I wound up at the altar rail.

As I knelt there it seemed like everyone in the church converged on me. They came out of the pews and stood around me at the altar rail where I was kneeling. I tried to pray, but there was too much distraction as everyone else in the church seemed to be praying out loud. I waited until things calmed down and returned to my seat.

But nothing had changed inside me. I was just the same as I had been—only a little more confused. They were good people, wanting to help. But running me through the wine press when I was not only green but still clinging to the vine accomplished nothing. I thanked Connie for taking me to church, but inwardly I determined not to go back.

Three days later we left for Germany on a major concert tour. I carried Helen's *Living Bible* with me, but I was afraid to open it, afraid it would devastate me.

Kim had gone to Texas with Mickey before I left for Germany. When I returned to the States, I flew directly to Texas to be with them for Christmas. Mickey's folks had moved from Anson to the little town of Wink in West Texas. I joined Mickey there, and we stayed with his folks who had no idea of the impending divorce. It was a difficult week, pretending everything was all right between us, but I knew when I left them on New Year's Day that it was all over between Mickey and me.

The nearest airport to Wink was at Midland, 75 miles away. I had to be in Shreveport that night for a performance. Mickey drove us to the airport. Kim slept most of the way, her head on my lap, her feet in Mickey's. It was time to start facing things.

Yet we were silent. I could see the tears trickling down Mickey's face. I was sitting on my side of the front seat, feeling completely desolate. But neither of us made an effort to reach out to the other. The flat countryside, broken only by the rolling tumbleweeds and low mesquite, flashed by outside. Over and over Helen's words kept running through my mind: "Why don't you pray for God's will to be your will?" But I was afraid.

I knew I was disobeying God. I knew most of all I was hurting Mickey. But I couldn't seem to help it. All those nights with him watching TV while I wanted to be held, to be loved; all those times in the kitchen when I had tried to put my arms around him, and he had backed off. If there had ever been any love, it had been squeezed out of me. I was dry.

I don't know why, but it seems that every critical point in my life has been surrounded with music. On that lonely ride from Wink to Midland it was Sammi Smith's "Help Me Make It Through the Night" coming through on the car radio. I was drawing my direction, my moods, my strength, my feelings from the sad words and melodies of country music.

Without love, though, I had lost my desire to sing and did so only when on stage. There was no music in my heart anymore. I was drained. My mind told me I should be writing my own music. Instead I was always singing someone else's songs. Shelby had his writers, and he planned what I sang. I was being made into his image, wearing what he wanted, singing what he told me to.

Margaret Lewis and Myra Smith wrote most of my songs: "Oh, Singer," "Country Girl," "There Never Was a Time We Didn't Love." They were true country, the kind which caught my mood, but Shelby insisted that some of my lyrics be suggestive. When I complained, he'd say, "Sing it anyway. You're not the one buying the records."

So I sang them anyway, but how I yearned for the day when I would have the courage to say, "I'm not comfortable with that song. I won't sing it." But I couldn't do that any more than I could tell Mickey Riley that I would love him simply because it was the right thing to do.

I said good-by to Mickey on the bright concrete apron at the Midland airport. We stood at the waist-high retaining wall. Mickey was holding Kim. The bitter, cold, Texas wind stung my ears and blew my long hair back over my shoulder. My eyes were burning, watering. I looked at Mickey. His shock of brown hair protruded from the cowboy hat pushed down on his head. Kim's head was on his shoulder, her little face almost hidden in the upturned collar of her coat.

It was time to go. Tears glistened on Mickey's face, and Kim reached up and touched one with her finger. I took her from him. She gripped my hand as we walked through the bright New Year's Day sunlight to the steps of the plane.

The words of one of my songs ran through my mind.

Take me back, oh singer,
Take me back.
I'm livin' a life I can't slow down
Except with a song.*

The door of the plane closed, and we taxied out on the runway, heading east toward Dallas, Shreveport, and God only knew where else. Wherever I was going, except for Kim, I was going alone. I gripped her hand, took a deep breath and wondered if there was anyone out there who would walk with me.

*"Oh, Singer" © 1971 Shelby Singleton Corp. Words and music by Lewis and Smith.

14

Limbo

*I*f I thought living with Mickey Riley was impossible, living without him was hell. And I didn't take long to find my place in the center of the inferno.

I can hardly believe the advice I got from my friends. Shelby Singleton, always blunt and true to his standards, thought Mickey was a fine fellow, but his concern was that I keep working.

"Mickey ought to take you over his lap and paddle your butt," he said. "But since you're going to do what you want to do, you might as well quit dilly-dallying around causing problems for all of us and get the divorce over with. Go ahead, harden your heart, and make it stick."

It was straight, worldly advice. But to listen I had to quench that little voice inside me that kept saying it was wrong. I remembered what Mama had said about the heifer on the rope. Instead of holding on, God seemed to have turned me loose on a long leash and was letting me wander around through hell. I kept wondering when He was going to jerk the other end.

Roger Morgan seemed to appear in my life out of a whirlwind. He had been my bass guitar player and road manager for my band, The Harper Valley Express. I first began to pay attention to him on the trip to Germany. But it quickly grew to be more.

Roger fit the quiet, poetic, romantic image I had always looked for in a man. His broad shoulders, narrow hips and dark skin gave him a mysterious, romantic look. Even though he was dapper, with an immaculate, continental look, he loved to wear a leather jacket and ride a motorcycle. It enhanced his macho image. But it was his eyes—deep chocolate marbles with long, spidery eyelashes—which fascinated me.

The more I was around him—on the bus, at our performances, spending time at his apartment or with him in my house—the more I felt he was the most gorgeous man I'd ever met. But there were a lot of things in him that disturbed me. He liked to drink hard liquor and had just begun to experiment with marijuana. Still I thought I saw gold beneath the surface, and it was a challenge to me to try to find a way to refine him into just the right kind of man to meet all my needs.

Roger's marriage was already in trouble, meaning he was just as vulnerable as I. We began to spend a lot of time together. It was a sticky situation. Roger and Nanette were sleeping in separate bedrooms. He kept telling me he was going to divorce her, that she was just a stopover wife after his first marriage. Even so, they were doing what Mickey and I had done—making a pretense at marriage until the divorce came through.

On several occasions they even invited me over for dinner. Nanette fixed steaks and then stayed in the kitchen to clean up while Roger and I went into the living room to talk. Nanette, though, was a walking powder-keg. I was too naive to realize I was the one playing with matches.

Roger had a dummy fireplace in his apartment. It presented a warm, cozy image, especially when there was snow on the ground outside. We would sit for long hours on the floor of his apartment. Nanette, finished in the kitchen, would storm through and say, "I'm going out. You two can stay here and talk 'business.'" Roger would joke about it, and I didn't care. I was back in love—with love.

He enjoyed burning candles, especially the scented kind. All this appealed to my senses. He would put soft rock on the record player or stuff like Jose Feliciano or James Taylor. I bought "Crosby, Stills, Nash and Young" and began to slip into those musical moods with Roger. The music touched my ears. The fragrance of vanilla and sandalwood candles touched my nose. The psychedelic light box, connected to the stereo player so it flashed soft, colored lights in designs of circles, squares and darts, appealed to my sight. The wine provided the taste, and Roger's lips were there to touch. Every sense was fulfilled. Only my spirit remained empty.

But it was not all pleasant. One afternoon we had checked into Vancouver, Washington, for a show. After the show Roger and I and another couple came back to the hotel suite where Roger introduced me to marijuana. The men rolled out the "joints" in cigarette papers, the woman watching intently. Roger wasn't a real cowboy like Mickey, I thought. He was a drugstore cowboy who mixed blue jeans with psychedelic shirts. Already he resented my wearing cowboy boots. It reminded him of my old days with Mickey. He was going to introduce me to a "new way of life," he said.

So we smoked. I took only a few drags on the skimpy little cigarette filled with crushed marijuana leaves, and something happened—something not pleasant at all. Suddenly the room turned around. Roger and the others all began to move in strange sequence. I could see the worried looks on their faces, anxiety as they stared at me, but I couldn't hear them. I realized something was happening to me, and suddenly I was standing up on the bed on the other side of the room, looking down on everyone, reaching my arms through the ceiling, through the roof, all the way to eternity. It was as though I had suddenly touched God and could now see as He saw. I saw them all the way they really were, and it scared me. I began to scream at the top of my voice.

The others were trying to pull me off the bed which had by now become a mountain. I was fighting them off, but I realized their sole purpose in life was to pull me down to their level. Now the entire room became a mountain— the back side of a mountain. I heard myself say to them, "Nothing is what I thought it was."

"What do you mean?"

"It's just not what I thought it was. I can see. I can see you. I *know* you," I said, pointing at each one of them.

They thought I was tripping out, but I realize now that for that brief moment I had eaten of the tree of knowledge and could see and discern.

"You all aren't even what I thought you were," I said. "You think you are my friends, but really you are not. I'm just somebody that you latched onto. You think you're really my friends, but you don't really even like me. You just like what I have."

I pointed at Roger. "And him," I spat out, "he's not even here. I see right through him. He's nothing."

I was really reaching, standing on the bed, groping for heaven. I was feeling what they were feeling, sensing what they were sensing.

"What are you doing?" Roger cried.

"I'm climbing this mountain," I said, kicking at them to keep them away from me. "There is something up there I've got to see. I don't know what it is. I think but I don't know. I'm afraid of it, but I'm drawn to it." All the time I was clawing at the wall, trying to climb to the ceiling from where I was standing on the bed. Then, as if I had suddenly broken through a cloud layer, I saw the top of the mountain.

I began to cry almost hysterically. "I can see it. I can see it. They're waiting for me."

"Who's waiting for you?" someone said.

"It's Mickey. It's Mickey and little Kim. They're on top of the mountain waiting for me." I fell against the wall, sobbing.

I felt an arm around my shoulder. "Maybe that's truth, Jeannie," the other man said as he helped me down and let me sit on the side of the bed. "Maybe in all this dope, you've seen something true."

They eventually went back to their rooms. But I didn't sleep any that night. The acrid smell of the marijuana lingered in the room, but even more real was the hellish vision: Mickey and Kim on top of the mountain, waiting for me. I knew I had to climb that mountain. I would never be fulfilled until I had scaled the peak and was where I belonged.

The next day we had a show in Ida Grove, Iowa, at the Ida County Fair. I don't know how I got up in the morning, much less got packed and to the airport. Everything was in a blur. Having talked with a number of people who have smoked marijuana, it seems what I went through the night before and then the next morning was a somewhat abnormal reaction to the drug. With all the emotional stress, I had just tripped out.

I couldn't get dressed that morning. I got out of bed, and it seemed the floor was 50 feet below the bed. Nita came and dressed me, combed my hair and helped me downstairs and into the taxi for the ride to the airport.

My bus met us in Ida Grove. Again, I couldn't function. It took forever in my room in the bus to get dressed. Nita had to pick out my clothes, fix my hair, do my thinking for me. All I could do was sit on the side of the bunk and mumble.

I tried to remember the lyrics to "There Never Was a Time," but it was all jumbled. "There was a time you'd sit in the backyard because the house would get so hot . . . the summer sun . . ." And I was off, trying to sing some kind of nonsense lyrics to a tune I made up.

I could shake myself back to reality but only for a few moments.

There was no way I could do the show that night. I thought, *Maybe when I get to the stage I will think real hard, and the words to the songs will come to mind.* But I couldn't even remember the lines to "Harper Valley PTA." I could see myself being led from the stage, babbling like a freaked-out druggy, and I would be through. Ruined. Forever.

Suddenly I was on stage before more than 3,000 people in the big open field at the fair. Everyone was applauding, and I was smiling. The band was already playing, and I picked up the mike to sing my opening song. I had sung that song hundreds of times.

But instead I missed even the first line. I freaked out. I made up words just to finish the line. I was a goner.

It all happened in a split second, the mind racing a million miles an hour ahead of the scene. I knew I was finished. And I prayed for the second time in a concert.

Oh, God, I don't deserve it, but sing this show for me.

And suddenly I was back on stage in Ida Grove and the words to the raunchy song—that song which in no way can be a God-honoring song—came flowing through my mouth.

I didn't miss another word. Not one note. I finished the show to a standing ovation and came back to encore a couple of songs I'd done only once or twice. I am still mystified over the grace of a God big enough to inspire me to sing something I know now He surely disapproved of. There is only one explanation that makes sense to me. He was willing for me to go on stage and sing a bunch of trash that didn't do anything but excite people in a fleshy way, simply because He loved me. In the years that followed, years of constant traveling, singing, trying to regain the top musical position from which I had fallen, I never forgot that miracle on the stage at the Ida County Fair when God intervened in my life.

The next four years passed in a frenzy of events and emotions. Mickey moved back to Nashville and had a service station at 21st and Grand on Music Row. He was living in an apartment. I saw him often. I would make an excuse just to drive by the service station, telling him I just "happened" to be in that section of town. I didn't want to live with him, but I was concerned about him. He was drinking too much. He wasn't taking care of himself. I was concerned for him but not concerned enough to love him "as an act of my will."

If I didn't go by the service station, Mickey would come by the house. Sometimes it was to pick up Kim. Sometimes it was to stay for supper. On Mother's Day and Easter he would drive to the top of the hill, honk, and Kim would come running back to the house with corsage boxes—one for her and one for me. In fact, it seemed as if Mickey paid more attention to me after we were divorced than when we were married. But I never dated him, and I never let him touch me. Sometimes he would call in the middle of the night and say, "Do you know there is a flight to Acapulco for breakfast?" I would laugh and kid with him, but never did I take him up on the idea. If we argued, he would often make up by sending a dozen red roses the next morning—by special courier.

Mickey was intensely jealous of Roger, but he seemed resigned to let events happen. "Go ahead and marry him," he told me once. "You may have to marry 10 men. It may be 20 years from now, but you'll be back with me. I'll wait, but don't expect me to wait alone."

I refused to think about that. Roger had become number one. And while Mickey was Kim's daddy, he was no longer my husband. I was free to make my own decisions. And I had decided on Roger.

Yet, as our relationship progressed, I began noticing small things about him that I didn't like—always comparing him with Mickey. Mickey had a healthy attitude toward money. I often remembered that terrible money fight in the London hotel room. Mickey really didn't care about money. If he had it, he spent it. If he didn't have it, he adjusted just as easily. He never seemed to worry about the lack of money nor did he spend lavishly if he didn't have it. He never wasted it by just pitching it out the window.

On the other hand, Roger did pitch it out the window. He was the most giving person I had ever seen, but his giving had no limits. He even gave when he didn't have it. He was constantly in debt. One day at the office he told me he was broke. He owed more than $3,000, and the finance company had just repossessed his motorcycle. That afternoon he went to town, bought a $300 leather jacket and charged it. He would buy, buy, buy. And when his furniture was repossessed he would go to another store and buy again. He just didn't seem to realize that money didn't come out of the ground with the spring crocuses, waiting for him to bend over and pick it up.

When Mickey sent me roses, they would last for weeks. But Roger's roses would wilt in a couple of days. Even the cookies that Mickey and Kim would make together lasted without molding.

Although I didn't realize it, I was contrasting the two men—Roger and Mickey—in every way. Mickey always seemed to come out on top.

Sometimes, though, his jealousy would irritate me. One night he called me on the phone and demanded to know where Roger was. I could tell he was likkered up and angry. I told him Roger was at his apartment.

"Well, I think it's about time that old boy stopped messing around with my wife. I'm going over there and call him out and thrash him good."

I reacted. "Listen here, Mickey Riley. You stay out of my life. And Roger's, too. I'm not your wife anymore, and I've got every right in the world to see who I want to see."

"Like hell you ain't my wife. No little piece of paper can take that away from me," he shouted.

We argued with each other for awhile over the phone, and I finally hung up. I heard later that Mickey got in his car and spent half the night driving around Roger's apartment, but nothing ever came of it. And deep inside, I was pleased Mickey still cared enough to fight for me.

15

The Life Line

*S*omething was happening to me. I had lost the desire to sing. I was doing it out of habit and because I needed the money. I had overextended myself financially. We had a new bus. Travel expenses were increasing. And good back-up musicians were expensive. I was singing now because I had to.

My brother-in-law, Gene, helped work out a deal so I would not have to pay the salaries of a full-time band. We contracted with a group called The Homesteaders who agreed to play only when I needed them, and they could freelance the rest of the time. I also let the rest of my old staff go, including Ron and Nita. I missed Nita especially, but Jackie Monaghan, who had been Brenda Lee's press coordinator, was now working for me full time as a press secretary. She arranged interviews and wrote press releases. More and more she was becoming my closest friend and confidante.

The new Silver Eagle bus was my way of keeping up with the country-music Joneses. Often it was just my driver, Curtis Cothron, Roger and myself rolling across the country—traveling in style in the latest Harper Valley Express.

I took every engagement that came along. Television shows, state fairs, a few concerts with other big-name singers and some night clubs, dinner clubs and joints. I sang for the county and regional fairs and the little podunk villages that could pay my fee. A lot of them could, simply because I was still a big name and drew a crowd. I only knew I was moving too fast to stop.

I began to wonder how many places would book me back the second time. Did they think I had only one good shot to give—"Harper Valley PTA"?

Robert Hilburn, critic for the *Los Angeles Times,* hurt me the most. At the time he wrote his scathing critique, I resented what he did to my professional career, but later I came to realize he was only telling the truth as he saw it at the time.

It was now late 1971, and I was in a concert at the Shrine Auditorium in Los Angeles. Ray Price, his Cherokee Cowboys and a huge orchestra were there. So were the Everly Brothers with their fine professional showing. The surprise of the evening was the Stonemans—an unknown group that almost stole the show. But I was the big headliner with my miniskirt, flashy boots, showing lots of cleavage and singing "Harper Valley PTA."

The next morning Hilburn's column in the *Times* had a black headline which read: "Little Talent." "Jeannie C. Riley has all the confidence in the world but, unfortunately, very little of the talent," he wrote. "First of all, her voice isn't any good. Second, neither is her material. That's two strikes against her. And as soon as the public forgets 'Harper Valley PTA,' that's strike three and she's out."

The truth was that I was slipping professionally. I was having to memorize the chatter between songs because I didn't trust myself to ad lib. I didn't have anything worthwhile to share. Other professional singers and entertainers were able to flow easily from one song to another. Everything I did was mechanical. But there was nothing routine about the steady drumbeat of spiritual happenings in my life.

I was in the dressing room at WLAC, Channel 5, in Nashville, to tape a segment for the TV show, "Hee-Haw." Connie Smith was there to tape also. I had already been on stage for one taping and came back to the dressing room and saw Connie sitting in a chair getting her hair fixed.

We made light conversation, then I noticed the cross she was wearing around her neck—a dainty, gold cross studded with diamonds.

"That's the prettiest cross I've ever seen," I said.

She touched it with her fingers. "Would you wear it if I gave it to you?"

"Oh, no, I couldn't," I said, backing off. "I didn't mean I wanted it. I was just admiring it on you."

"I want you to have it," she said. "I think the Lord would have me give it to you. I want to wear it while I'm taping my next song. Then, if you'll wait, I'll give it to you."

I was embarrassed and tried to say no again, but she just brushed it aside and went on out to the studio.

A diamond cross from Connie Smith! Half of me wanted to take it, but the other half knew I shouldn't. I felt guilty even thinking about it. I knew she was having a hard time financially. I also suspected some of it was because she had taken her stand as a Christian. Even more reason why I couldn't take the cross. But a few minutes later she was back in the dressing room. She brushed past me to collect her things, and I felt relieved. She had just said it to be nice. Now I wouldn't have to be under obligation by accepting such a beautiful gift. Then I heard Connie say, "Oh! I nearly forgot." I looked up and she was taking the cross off her neck.

I began to back up. "No, Connie, I can't."

"But you must," she said, smiling. "A lot of people have given me crosses since I became a Christian. I don't feel I can give them away since they were gifts. But this one I bought for myself, and so I can therefore give it to you."

Then she smiled again. "But since it's a gift, that means you can't give it away either. You've got to keep it forever, just to remind you that the gift of Jesus Christ is the most precious gift in the world."

I felt the tears coming and tried to force them back. "Oh, Connie, I can't wear this. It's too nice."

"It's not the cross, Jeannie," she said, hanging it around my neck. "It's the Man who came down from the cross that's important."

So I took it. Giving away money had been easy for me.

I had always bought expensive presents for others. I had given my sister Helen a whole room full of furniture, bought a washing machine and dryer for Mama, purchased expensive gifts for Roger. But to give away something I had bought for myself? That was something else. Especially to hang it around another singer's neck—a rival singer at that. Connie had something special, something I didn't have, something I needed desperately.

Long after Connie had gone I stood in front of the mirror of the dressing room fingering the cross which now hung from my neck. "Love is something you do," Daddy had said that night at the house when Mickey and I were battling so furiously. I had just seen that in action.

Three weeks later I purchased an entire tray of special perfumes for Connie. In my imagination I pictured myself pouring them on her head like the woman of the street had poured the perfume on Jesus. But that seemed foolish, so I took them to the gift-wrap counter at an exclusive department store in Nashville. I finally picked out some sand-colored wrapping paper decorated with blue camels. The clerk suggested I top it off with a blue flower.

"Why would I want to put a flower in the desert?" I joked. Then suddenly I felt the mist in my eyes. That's what Connie Smith was to me—a flower in the desert.

I grabbed an old piece of wrapping paper and quickly wrote down the lyrics as they poured through my head. I knew the song was to be a very personal one—and that some day I would find the nerve to call Connie on the phone and sing it to her.

> On this earthly desert, praying for a drop of rain,
> I saw a flower blooming midst my thirst and hunger
> pains . . .
> She was a flower in the desert
> And I kept wondering why
> She was always in full bloom
> While I was withered dry.
> And seeking the oasis that kept her in supply,
> There I found eternal springs of life . . .
> Eternal life.

Something had begun to happen in Kim. I had been reading *The Living Bible* to her. It was one of the few times we had together. At bedtime I would listen to her prayers. They were always the same: "Dear God, please send Daddy back to live with us." It was a heartbreaking prayer, especially since I didn't want it to come to pass. But that didn't seem to bother Kim at all. She kept right on praying, often asking me, "Mama, when do you think God will send Daddy home?"

Mickey had never been totally out of my life, of course. Sometimes he would stop by in the evening if he knew I was home, and I would fix him bacon and eggs. If he kept Kim on the weekends, he would often linger and talk in the kitchen or the living room. I enjoyed having him around, but I was afraid he might show up the same time Roger was there. The thing I feared most, I think, was an encounter between them—in my presence.

When Mickey was in the house, I would take the phones off the hook, fearful Roger might call. I knew if he came by and saw Mickey's car in the driveway, he wouldn't stop. But even a phone call might set Mickey off, and I did everything possible to prevent any kind of contact.

One Sunday night Mickey brought Kim home, stayed for supper and then hung around as I put her to bed. Again Kim prayed that little prayer: "Dear God, I'm so happy Daddy is here. Please let him come back to live with us."

I looked up, and Mickey had tears in his eyes. So did I. We tucked Kim into bed and went into my big bedroom to talk. I deliberately kept the lights low so he could not spot Roger's picture on my dressing table. We sat in the chairs on the other side of the room and Mickey talked.

"You know, one day we'll be back together again."

"Mickey, let's not talk about it. We've been through it so many times already. It just won't work out. I love you, but I don't have the right feeling for you."

Thirty minutes after Mickey left, Roger was at the door. While he was there things were glamorous, but after he left and I would wake in the morning, it was always the same thought: "You're not my husband. You don't belong here."

When I was four years old, Mama took me down to Sullivan's 5 & 10 cent store in Anson. She had a nickel and told me to look around—that I could have anything a nickel would buy. I picked out a little toy, but on the way out of the store I spotted a little, flesh-colored rubber doll, no bigger than the palm of my hand. I picked it up, too, but hid it in my hand until we were out on the sidewalk. Then, in joyful innocence, I opened my hand and showed Mama what I had done.

"Look what I've got, Mama," I grinned.

She grabbed me by the shoulder, marched me back in the store, and made me give the doll back to Mary Lee Sullivan who was behind the counter.

I never stole again from a store. Yet here I was, with the same kind of innocence, trying to justify stealing another woman's husband.

My frustrations drove me back to the Bible. Not only was I reading it to Kim; I began taking *The Living Bible* with me on trips. I was surprised. I could actually understand what it was all about. One day, sitting on a plane I remarked to myself, "Well, I can't believe this. I can actually understand what I'm reading." I finished the book of John and went back to the first book in the New Testament, Matthew. Then I read Luke. I was dismayed how similar they were. It had never dawned on me the four Gospels were all the same story, the life of Jesus written from different men's perspective. That's how dumb I was. I told Helen and Gene of my discovery, and they laughed.

"That's just further proof of the Bible confirming itself," they said. "Keep on reading and see what you discover."

But when it came to places in the Bible such as ". . . a man should leave his father and mother, and be forever united to his wife" (Matthew 19:5,TLB), I quickly skipped over them. That teaching was something I wasn't prepared to accept—even if it was in the Bible.

Something else began to happen. Maybe it was because of Kim's prayers. But if I was on the road on Sunday morning, I always got up early and turned on the TV to watch the preachers. Often, if I was alone in the room, I would get on my knees in front of the TV set and pray along with the preacher on the tube, sometimes repeating his prayer word for word. I wanted God desperately. I wanted Him the way Connie Smith had Him. But I didn't want Him so badly that I was willing to change my way of life. I just couldn't. And when I thought about having to give up Roger or to take Mickey back: well that was too much. I would get up off my knees and switch the TV set to another channel.

Sometimes I would get up from my knees thinking, *Well, I prayed it but nothing happened.* Then I would think that the reason nothing happened was because I was unwilling to give up Roger. But I knew I couldn't do that because I didn't have the strength. So I just figured I was bound for hell, no matter what.

Even Roger, who was waiting for his divorce from Nanette to go through, seemed to respect my quest. He wasn't aware of the inner struggle I was going through to give him up, of course. He just thought an old-fashioned, Christian girl would be the best thing in the world as his wife—just as long as he didn't have to accommodate himself to her faith.

Reading the Bible, however, was beginning to have an effect on my life at a level I couldn't visualize, much less comprehend. This, combined with a series of unexplainable circumstances, was driving me deeper and deeper into personal anxiety. Countless times I would wake up in the middle of the night, my digital clock reflecting 1:11 a.m. I would lie in bed thinking, *Three ones: that's Mickey, Kim, and me.* My Bible would fall open to verses like Hebrews 11:1. I wouldn't read the verse because all I could see was those three ones. I felt I was being tormented by outside forces designed to destroy me.

Gene and Helen were attending Forest Hills Baptist Church in Nashville with regularity. I began going with them since Helen was teaching a Sunday school class. And on April 2, 1972, at a morning service, something in me finally snapped. The preacher mentioned a particular passage of Scripture in his sermon which seemed to set off a chain of events. The verse was: "Behold, I stand at the door, and knock: if any man hear my voice, and open the door, I will come in to him, and will sup with him, and he with me" (Revelation 3:20).

I thought, *I know He's been knocking. I've gotten down on my knees and said I wanted Him to save me from myself, from my sins. But I haven't been able to give up what I thought He wanted me to give up. But He says if I just open the door, He will come in. I don't have to change anything. I don't have to throw out any of the old furniture. I don't even have to rearrange it. All I have to do is open the door and ask Him to come in.*

Then another verse of Scripture ran through my mind, one of the verses I had read as a child, and I had read it recently in my Bible study. ". . . if thou shalt confess with thy mouth the Lord Jesus, and shalt believe in thine heart that God hath raised him from the dead, thou shalt be saved" (Romans 10:9). Sitting there in the pew of that beautiful church, I let my mind race ahead of the sermon. *All I have to do is confess with my mouth and believe Jesus is the Son of God.* The Bible didn't say anything about the Rogers in my life, it didn't say anything about getting things right with my husband—or rather ex-husband. All it said was to believe Jesus is the Son of God and say it with my mouth. Well, I could certainly do that. I could open the door and let Him in. Then if He wanted to do any changing, it was up to Him—not me. The only thing left for me to do was to answer the preacher's invitation, go down to the front of the church and confess that Jesus was my Lord. If I did that, I would be saved and wouldn't go to hell—which was all I was concerned about at that time.

I had just finished my reverie when the pastor gave an invitation, inviting all those who wanted to accept Jesus Christ to come to the front of the church. I did it!

Even as I made those first steps down the aisle, something began happening in me: a quick ecstasy, like warm syrup, seemed to be poured over me. I didn't know what had happened. All I knew was that I had been obedient to the voice within, and suddenly I had the assurance I was saved.

That morning, after the service as I was going out the door, I was stopped by a tiny little woman in her late 80s whom everybody called Granny Phillips. She congratulated me on my decision and then said something prophetic.

"You're a beautiful girl, and you seem real sweet. But the

Lord has told me to tell you something."

I didn't know the Lord spoke to people like that, so immediately I was listening. I had just made a profession of my faith in Jesus Christ and was feeling warm all over. Now here comes an old woman who certainly looked like what I imagined a prophetess would look like, and she stood in front of me with a personal message from the Lord.

"What is it, ma'am?"

"You are supposed to go back to Mickey and be a wife to him and be a mother to your little girl."

"How'd you know my husband's name?" I asked, startled.

"He was here two years ago," she said. "I saw him right back there in the very back pew. He was holding that little girl on his lap. The Lord told me then he was your husband and that he loves you very much."

I began to shake, and I looked around for Helen to help me get away. But Helen was talking to people near the front of the church, and I was left alone with this old prophetess. She began to quote Scripture: "For this cause shall a man leave father and mother and shall cleave to his wife. Wherefore they are no more twain, but one flesh. What therefore God has joined together, let not man put asunder."

A series of electric shocks seemed to go through my body. I tried to be polite, but I didn't want to hear what she was saying. She was quoting all the Scriptures I had skipped over in my Bible reading, all the passages I hadn't underlined. I thanked her, asked her to pray for me and quickly moved away. She was calling after me. "Remember what I said. It is a word from God. Don't quench the Holy Spirit, Jeannie."

The next week was hell on earth. I felt I was on the devil's battlefield being tugged in one direction by the Spirit of God and in the other direction by Satan himself. The first thing I did was rush to Roger's apartment and share the wonderful news of my salvation. I was taken aback by his response: "Where does that leave me?"

When I told him I was going to be baptized the following Sunday night, he asked angrily, "Is Mickey going to be there?"

I told him I didn't know, but I thought he had a right to come if he wanted to. Roger replied with anger that if Mickey was going to be there, he wasn't going to come.

"But you've just got to come," I pleaded.

"Well, you find out if Mickey's going to be there. If he's not coming, then I'll go with you."

But Mickey was planning to attend. Granny Phillips had called him at the station early Monday morning and told him about my going forward in the church and insisted Mickey come for the baptism service. Mickey called me and said he was happy for me, and he wanted to sit with Kim in church while I was being baptized. When I called Roger back, he exploded.

"I sure ain't coming if he's going to be there," he said, and hung up the phone. I felt as if I was being stretched between two wild horses. Even at my baptism there was to be no peace.

Yet I knew something had happened deep inside me. It was as if I had been connected to a life line. Even though I was still in the giant whirlpool of the world's system, caught in my own cesspool of emotional attachments, I had touched life—and there was Someone on the other end of the life line, stronger even than the suction that had been pulling me downward, who was slowly pulling me to safety.

Mickey and Kim sat on the back pew while I was baptized. The next day I placed two telephone calls. One was to television evangelist Jimmy Swaggart. He was in Minnesota in a crusade. We had never met but he knew who I was. I had listened to my housekeeper play his records: "There Is a River," "Who Am I That a King Would Bleed and Die for?" "This Is Just What Heaven Means to Me." I wanted him to know his music—which had filled my house—had played a big role in my life.

The other call was to Bill Mack, an all-night disc jockey in Dallas, Texas. Bill had a live program which covered the Southwest. I hadn't been in contact with him for years. I wanted someone in Texas, however, to know I had become a Christian, someone who could get the word out to all my friends. I had done a show with Bill in Panther Hall, a "Big D" television jamboree, even before I came to Nashville.

He had been one of the first deejays to play "Harper Valley PTA." He was a friend of mine and Uncle Johnny's, and for some reason, maybe because it was always good business just to keep in touch with the deejays, I felt I should let him know. So I called Bill. He was on the air at the time and patched my phone call into the microphone. I gave my testimony to all of Texas—and a large portion of the nation—over WBAP in Dallas.

I didn't know it at the time, but that testimony was going to return to me in the form of an echo which would eventually change my life in more ways than I could ever dream.

16

Kind of Wonderful

*L*ess than two weeks had passed since I had called Bill Mack when I received a letter from the wife of a Nazarene pastor in Sidney, Nebraska. Her name was Carolyn Abke, and a friend had called her after hearing my testimony over the Dallas station to tell her I had become a Christian.

"First of all, let me say I'm not a fan of yours," she wrote. "I'm just not interested in country music. But I know who you are and have been praying for you for three years, ever since the Lord gave me a dream about you. You and I were standing on the back of a train. You kept trying to jump off, and I kept trying to pull you back. I kept reaching for you until my arms were exhausted. I was losing my grip but was grasping for your clothing. Your clothes were ripping, and you were almost gone. A handsome man appeared on the back of the train with us. I knew it was the devil in disguise. He told me, 'Let her go. It's too late. You can't save her.' I screamed at him, 'Oh, no, I can't let her go. She will be doomed forever.'

"I went to Sunday school that morning and told my class about the dream. We agreed to begin praying for you, by name, that you might be saved. All this time we have prayed for you, and now I understand you have become a Christian. A friend of mine called and said you were on a radio program and told them you had accepted Christ, and you told how your granddaddy was a Nazarene minister. I just thought it was kind of wonderful that the Lord would put you on this Nazarene heart of mine to pray for you all these years."

I was awestruck. I could feel the little hairs on my arms standing up on end as I read the letter. This unknown woman, the wife of Reverend Gary Abke in Nebraska, had been praying for me all these years. I wondered, *Is this the reason Helen had given me the Bible? Is this the reason these folks have been talking to me about Jesus? Is this the reason my clock has been stopping at 1:11?*

I wrote her back, thanking her for her prayers and asking her to keep on praying. If the Lord had answered that prayer, maybe He would answer other prayers also.

For I knew that my life was far from right in God's eyes. When I accepted Jesus into my life, I was told that the blood of Jesus Christ did wipe out my "sin." But it wasn't the "sin" that bothered me, it was the sins. And they were still plenty evident. What could I do about them?

Since I felt uncomfortable in my miniskirts, I started letting out the hems—an inch at a time. I began pulling my blouses up in the front and not showing so much cleavage. I abandoned my interest in astrology.

But what about Roger?

The night after my baptism I went by his place, and we had a long talk. He was hurt and confused by the change in my life. Secretly I was wishing he would say he could no longer have anything to do with me now that I was a Christian. Instead he left the decision to me—and I didn't know how to handle it.

One thing I did commit myself to was to break off our intimate relationship. I needed to find out if that relationship was built on anything more solid than the feelings we aroused in each other.

The pastor at the Baptist church said the first thing I should do was "get involved" in the church activities and learn to share my Christian faith with everyone. And so I began telling people, even perfect strangers, "It's easy. All you've got to do is get down on your knees and accept the

Lord. It's wonderful going to heaven and not going to hell."

How easily I had forgotten the struggle that had been mine before I reached the place of surrender. And all those lonely Sunday mornings in motel rooms when I knelt in front of the TV sets and did the same thing, only to arise and realize nothing had come of it.

Gradually I began to realize my efforts were fruitless. People were polite, and some even, for the sake of courtesy, did what I asked them to. With a few it was real. Yet I knew somehow that I was not ready to be a disciple. God still did not have my heart. The war in me between the Spirit and the flesh was very real. My resolutions, as good as they were, could not make me holy. Within three months I drifted back to Roger as before.

But there was no satisfaction in it. I was miserable. Guilt consumed me. I resented his being in my life, and I resented myself for not knowing what to do about it. I knew I was being deceived. I knew Roger was the handsome man who had appeared on the back of the train in Carolyn Abke's dream. I kept thinking, *If only he would become a Christian, then we would get married, and I could live in peace.* But Roger showed no signs of being interested in the Christian life.

Yet during this wretched time in my life an unexplainable thing happened. Jackie Monaghan, who had become such a close friend and was living with me much of the time, took a big step. Even though I was in a spiritual pit and could see only defeat, Jackie had seen where the victory was. She saw my struggles. She heard me cry—and pray. And even though I fell, she knew somehow there was a personal God out there who cared and reached for Him. She accepted Jesus Christ as Lord of her life.

Jackie and I were opposites in so many ways. She was taller, bigger than I was and almost jolly. She was single. Yet I found in her a friend in whom I could confide. She had a beautiful gift for listening and a heart for hoping. We were good for each other.

Then out of my twisted thinking came this prayer: *Lord, I have feelings for Mickey and for Roger. I don't know which one is the right one for me. So whichever one makes a decision for You first—that's the one I'll marry.*

It seemed a funny prayer at the time. I wasn't sure the Lord would go for such a bargain. I knew He wanted both Mickey and Roger to become Christians. And I didn't see how I could marry either of them unless they were. After all, how could I have a Christian home if my husband wasn't Christian?

Three months after I became a Christian, Kim walked down the aisle and told the preacher at the Baptist church that she wanted Jesus in her heart, too. She had seen something in me that convinced her little heart that I was changed. She began singing around the house, songs like: "I have decided to follow Jesus, no turning back, no turning back." There were other stanzas to the chorus:

> My cross I'll carry till I see Jesus . . .
> Though none go with me, still I will follow . . .

Mickey would call me, after she had been with him for the weekend. His voice was plaintive. "She's been over here singing those little songs," he said. "And she insists I listen to her say her prayers at night. What's happened to her?"

She was the same around me. Her prayers at night were filled with petitions to God: *"Dear God, I want Mommy and Daddy back together again." "I want a farm." "I want a pony." "I want to live with Mommy and Daddy on a farm."*

She was praying the same prayers at Mickey's knee, too. Occasionally Mickey would bring her to church. The Sunday night before I was to leave for an extensive concert tour of Europe, Mickey, Kim and I sat in church together. I had written him a love letter and sealed it in an envelope. The idea of dying without having fulfilled God's perfect plan for my life bothered me. Especially did I dread dying and leaving Mickey behind, wondering if I really loved him or not. So I had written him this note and told him to open it only if I were to die.

That night in church I sat silently in the pew beside Kim, bartering with God. *Lord, if only Mickey would answer the invitation at the end of the service. Then I would know he's safe and I would see him in heaven. If he would accept Christ tonight, then I could tell You before I leave on this trip that I would go back to him.*

The choir sang the invitation hymn, ironically the same one Kim had been singing around the house: "I have decided to follow Jesus, no turning back." I looked over at Mickey. His eyes were filled with tears. Suddenly he was out in the aisle, heading toward the altar. I began to cry. I grabbed Kim's hand, and we stood, barely able to catch our breath, as Mickey took the preacher's hand. *At last,* I thought, *now I know for sure.*

But Mickey had not gone forward to make a profession of faith in Christ. He had simply gone to transfer his church letter from the Hannah Baptist Church outside of Anson to the Forest Hills Baptist Church in Nashville. I kept hoping the preacher would ask him if he had committed his life to Jesus Christ, and if he hadn't, would he do it now. But there were no such questions. Instead, as was the custom in the Baptist church, the preacher asked the congregation to vote if they welcomed Mickey Riley into the organization of the church, and as usual there was unanimous approval.

I felt let down. I had so badly wanted Mickey to publicly profess Jesus Christ as his Savior. And he had gotten so close. He had been welcomed into the fellowship of the church, but no one seemed to wonder if he was a Christian or not. I left for Europe the next morning still confused. Was it to be Roger or Mickey?

I had been at the crossroads so long I was open to any kind of guidance. While I had rejected astrology as a guide for my life I had nothing to take its place. I began letting my Bible drop open and putting my finger at random on some verse, hoping this would give me direction. However, that just seemed to be another type of astrology, a sort of Biblical crystal-ball gazing. What did impress me was the increasing number of people who just seemed to "appear" in my life, all with the same message. Helen. Connie Smith, LaWayne Satterfield. Granny Phillips. A sales clerk in a department store stopped me in the aisle one afternoon. "Your ex-husband still loves you," she said, looking me in the eye. "God wants you to go back to him." I had never seen her before. It scared me so much I refused to go back in that store for a long time.

I was constantly breaking up with Roger—and going back. I would go down to Mickey's service station intending to tell him that if he would become a Christian I could come back to him, but then I'd find him drinking. We would get into a horrible shouting match, and I'd storm away, angry at God, Mickey, Roger and myself.

Just before my housekeeper left to accept another job, she took me with her to church services at The Lord's Chapel. This was a small group of people which had started as a weeknight prayer group and had grown into a church that met in the old Harding mansion off Highway 70. There was no beautiful building or fine furnishings. The beauty was in the people. They hugged each other. They clapped when they sang. And my, how they sang—never wanting to stop. They laughed. They cried. They prayed. They were different from any group of people I'd ever seen. They had life. And love.

I sat through the two-hour service, electrified by the spiritual power I sensed in the place. There were about 60 present, and everyone seemed to be taking part in the service. Some testified of the presence of God. Others talked about their changed lives. The pastor, whom everyone referred to as Brother Moore, was leading—yet he, too, seemed to be taking orders from Someone else. Over and over the people testified to the power of the Holy Spirit in their lives.

Somehow, after the service was over, I ended up in a side room with a number of young people and Brother Billy Roy Moore, the pastor. They gathered around the chair where I was sitting, put their hands on my head and shoulders and prayed. Someone said softly, "God wants you to know He loves you, Jeannie, just as you are. He has baptized you in His Holy Spirit. In the days ahead there will be great changes in your life. Do not fear them; the same God is going to lead you into a land of milk and honey."

I left the meeting in a daze, wondering what could possibly happen to me next.

Needing a housekeeper, I placed an ad in the paper asking for a lady to take care of Kim and do light housework. A number of people applied, but none of them seemed right.

I was supposed to leave town Thursday morning and still had no one by Tuesday night.

That night I prayed: *Lord, day after tomorrow morning I've got to leave town. I need someone to keep Kim. Please send me a miracle.*

As I was praying, I thought of Wilma Reid. Wilma was on the staff of Forest Hills Baptist Church. She was dainty and feminine, but she was not afraid of the hardest work. Her daughter, Phyllis, had made a road trip with me the summer before to baby sit with Kim. I had gotten to know her mother through that contact.

Now that's the kind of person I need, I said to the Lord. *Father, I'll know it's the right one if You send me someone like Wilma Reid. I'm gonna leave it in Your hands.*

All day Wednesday I was tempted to call one of the women who had applied earlier. But deep in my heart I knew none of them was right. That night precisely at 9 o'clock the doorbell rang. There on the front porch stood Wilma Reid.

"I've come to tell you I turned in my resignation at the church business meeting tonight," she said. "I knew you needed someone to help you, and since I love you and Kim so much, I just felt I should come around here and let you know I'm available."

I was too astonished to talk. Covered with goose bumps, I backed into the kitchen, stammering and trying to hold back the tears. I had asked for someone like Wilma Reid, and He had sent me Wilma herself. Though divorced from my husband, angry at God half of the time and often filled with bitterness and unforgiveness, He loved me enough to do this.

Wilma moved in early the next morning and stayed for three years—leaving only when she had to take care of her dying mother. She was like Solomon, full of wisdom and spiritual insight. She moved furniture, paid the bills and did most of the praying. I would often come home and find her out in the back yard, dressed in gold shoes, white lace blouse and wearing a fancy blonde wig—chopping wood for the fireplace. She was one of the greatest gifts the Lord has ever given me.

And there came this conviction: I knew I was going to have to get my life straightened out with God if I was to continue receiving His blessings. There was just no way I could always be on the receiving end of things. I wanted to be able to give like that, too.

17

Looking for a Miracle

*E*veryone had advice for me, it seemed: my parents, Helen, Jackie, Wilma, friends, even strangers. And of course there were Mickey and Roger. It was confusing.

Even Curtis Cothron, the driver of my bus—who to my knowledge was not a Christian—had a prophetic word for me. He had taken Kim and me around to Mickey's apartment where I had left my daughter to spend the weekend with her daddy. When I climbed back into the bus, Curtis leaned forward.

"You know, the way you've been reading that Bible and talking about God lately, I'll bet you and Mickey will be getting back together before long."

It was as though my becoming a Christian—even though I wasn't much of one—meant to everyone that my home would soon be back together again.

Wilma told me the Bible said love was a willful act. "How can the Bible demand that you love someone?" I argued. "It's not fair. No one can control love; it just happens."

"Honey, love ain't something you fall into, like a ditch or a hole. Love is something you do because God tells you to do it."

There it was again—Daddy's advice.

"I can't help it if I love Roger and don't love Mickey," I said, frustrated.

"Sure you can," Wilma said with a smile. "When God tells you to love your husband, you love him."

"But how?"

"By submitting to him for better or worse," she said seriously.

It was too much for me to understand.

Shortly thereafter I was on my bus heading for Kansas City and a two-night concert. Roger and Curtis were in the front. I was in my bedroom across the back of the bus with the door closed, praying.

Lord, I've reached the end of trying. I've read the Bible. I've listened to everyone. And now I'm so confused I can't even pray. I don't even know what to pray for. Just take over, Lord. You pray for me.

I was on my knees now, and the words began coming faster and faster until they were a steady stream—loud and wonderful. Praise. I had never praised God before. I had talked about Him and with Him. I had even told Him I loved Him. But praise . . . that was something different.

As the words streamed from my mouth, like a mountain brook following a spring rain, I began to have mental images of all the people I had touched in my life—and hurt. It began with my playmates in my childhood. Their faces seemed to flash on a screen in my mind, like slide projections. Then my parents. Mickey's friends who worked on the highway department. Phil. Harry. Shelby. Pete. Each vision would last for a few minutes as the torrent of words poured from me, and then it would fade to be replaced by another. I kept waiting for the spring to run dry, for the flow to decrease, but it kept going. Was this what Jesus was talking about in John 7 when He said, "Out of your belly shall flow rivers of living water"? I had read those verses over and over, but I did not understand them—until now.

Literally hundreds of images, people I had met only for a short while and then forgotten, flashed across my mind. As they appeared, it was as though my spirit recognized them with a joyful "yes!" Then I would be praying for them—or rather, the Holy Spirit would be praying for them through me. My prayer lasted two hours, and that night I slept with more peace than I had in years.

Spring arrived. To most it brought with it the spirit of fresh beginnings. Not to me. Everything was still in confusion. If I had thought several spiritual experiences would end all my problems, I was badly mistaken. The problems didn't disappear. If anything, they intensified.

Roger's divorce had been settled, and he was pressuring me to set a wedding date. I finally consented, only to back off. I just couldn't trust him. Some of my friends said he was using me. Others, folks in the church even, said God had spoken to them and that I was to marry Roger. Still others said I was to go back to Mickey. The confusion mounted.

Granny Phillips called. "Jeannie, I heard you were going to marry Roger. That's a mistake. There is only one man for you: the man God gave you to begin with."

Jackie Monaghan had moved into a new apartment, and it was Mickey who helped her with her furniture. I pulled up in her driveway and sat looking at my ex-husband. *Isn't that something?* I thought. *Why is he doing that for her when he knows that I may soon be marrying someone else?* Then I thought, *He's really not doing that for Jackie. He's doing it for me.*

Mickey came over to the car window. His blue denim shirt was soaked with sweat. He had torn the nail on one of his fingers, and it was covered with dried, caked blood. He leaned on the window sill.

"Are you going to let me take you and Kim to church on Easter morning?"

Kim was in the seat beside me. "Oh, yes, Mama. We can go and be a family."

I had no choice but to agree. Mickey grinned and said he'd pick us up at my house.

He brought us both flowers—beautiful corsages. It felt good to go with him to church, to pull up in the parking lot at Forest Hills Baptist Church and go into the building like normal people. After church we left the building and started walking across to the car. I spotted Granny Phillips on the sidewalk. She had been in a home for the elderly and had come to the church that morning for the first time in a long while.

"Oh, Mickey, we've just got to say hi to her. She hasn't seen you since you joined the church a year ago."

"Nobody much has seen me," he grinned. "I've only been back once since then."

I grabbed his hand and pulled him toward Granny Phillips. She hugged his neck and said something like it was "meant" for us to stop and talk. Then she hobbled off on her cane. We got into our car to drive home.

Mickey took us straight to my house on Stonewall Jackson Court. Just as he was turning off Granny White Pike onto our street, I saw a motorcycle coming. It turned down Stonewall Jackson just before we reached the corner. As we pulled in behind it I saw to my horror that it was Roger. He was heading for my house up the hill on the dead-end street. Had he come later and seen Mickey's car in the driveway, he would have gone on past. But he didn't see it was us until he pulled up in front of my house and cut his engine. We pulled around him and into the driveway. Mickey saw him first, and I knew it had ruined his perfect Easter with Kim and me. Had we been two minutes earlier, we could have avoided the confrontation. But we had stopped to speak to Granny Phillips. Now this.

I jumped out of the car and went flying back down the driveway to try to explain to Roger. Roger couldn't talk. He was so upset his cheeks were going in and out.

"I know what I saw," he said through shaking lips. "I saw a man and his wife and child go by in a car. I don't care what you say, you're still married to him."

I tried to get hold of his arm, but he jerked it away and screamed, "Leave me alone. I don't belong in this. I'm the extra man." He cranked up his bike and roared off.

When I turned around, Mickey was already in the house with Kim. I ran in the house and met Mickey coming out the front door. He was supposed to stay for dinner, but he threw the car keys at me.

"Here's the keys," he snapped. "If you want him, go get him."

We were supposed to have an Easter-egg hunt for Kim. But this had spoiled everything. Mickey drove away. Alone. Leaving Kim with my housekeeper, I jumped in the car and drove to Roger's apartment. He wasn't there so I waited. He finally came in, stormed around, smashed his brass lamp against the wall, swore and told me to leave.

"I'll find somebody else better than you," he said as I left.

But by the end of the week, Roger had calmed down. We talked again, and I finally set the date for a June wedding. I called Mickey.

"Do what you must," he said, "But one day you'll be back. And I'll be waiting."

That made things difficult. Roger's actions didn't help either. A friend told me that he had been seen with one of the strippers at the Red Lion Lounge. It was just enough to make me cancel the wedding date. Confused, Roger resigned from the band and returned to New England to live near his parents.

Even though I was sad, there was a lifting of my spirits. I felt I was free of something that had been hung around my neck for years. *Maybe,* I thought, *I'll now feel something for Mickey.*

But nothing had changed. I waited, even prayed for a special feeling—some way I could know I was in love with Mickey. But there was nothing. No goose bumps, no wildly beating heart, not even much of a desire to be around him. Things seemed more hopeless than ever.

18

Crisis

*I*t was early October. Everything in Nashville was alive with autumn color, filled with music. Everything but me. Even with Roger out of my life I was colorless. Someone told me that when I accepted Christ all my questions should have been answered, all my problems should have been over. I would begin to bloom, they said. Well, I did bloom— but my blossoms were surrounded by thorns. It seemed every problem I had before I became a Christian had accompanied me into my new life. Try as I might, I was unable to find answers to most of the big questions surrounding me.

One Sunday morning at The Lord's Chapel, Billy Roy Moore preached on "crisis." He said crisis was God's means of getting our attention, and the Christian should be thankful for it. In fact, he said, the Christian should be thankful for all things—even the things which brought pain and confusion. I had a hard time reconciling that with what others were saying: that God was a God who relieved pain, not a God who sent it. And what should I do with the Scripture that said God was not the author of confusion? If all that was so, then why all this inner pain and confusion? Was there still something missing? Could it be that the problems stemmed from who I was, rather than what I did?

Then, as the final ingredient in my stew of confusion, Roger's sister called from New Hampshire. There had been no word from him since he left in July. I honestly believed he was out of my life. Now this phone call.

"Has Roger gotten there yet?"

"What do you mean? I asked, startled.

"Well, he's gotten himself straightened up and is on his way back to Nashville. I thought you knew."

I panicked. I hung up the phone, got in my car and drove down to Mickey's service station. I had to see him. Was Mickey the one? Or was I to go back to Roger? I had to know.

But Mickey had been drinking that day. His life seemed so miserable. He was not eating correctly. His eyes were bloodshot, and his tongue rolled around in his mouth when he tried to talk. I stayed only a moment and drove away, crying.

It just didn't seem possible that God would be requiring me to love him in that shape. Surely if He had someone for me, it would be a man fully dedicated to the cause of Christ.

Roger knocked on my door at 11 a.m. the next day. He was even more handsome than I remembered. He had been on a salad and steak diet, living in a cabin behind his parents' house, breathing fresh country air and "communing with nature" which he equated with God.

"I've done a lot of thinking," he said, helping himself to a cup of spiced tea in my kitchen. "I'm a fool to let a girl like you get by me. You said the only thing standing in our way was my relationship with God. Now I'm ready to make things right with Him."

He looked so good. I knew his convictions needed to be tested to see if they were real, but it all sounded like just what God wanted for me. Seeing Mickey drunk the day before and now seeing Roger looking like he had just stepped out of the Bible—it all seemed to be fitting into place.

For the next six weeks I watched Roger. He had a room in a boarding house and had taken a job as a busboy at Jay's Steak House. Sometimes in the evening I would go by just to watch him at work in his white uniform cleaning tables and carrying dirty dishes. It made me respect him even more. He had changed. It was obvious.

On Sundays Roger would pick me up and take me to church at The Lord's Chapel. He seemed genuinely interested in spiritual things. He talked to Brother Moore and said he wanted to be baptized as a believer. He also wanted the pastor to marry us.

Roger came out of the baptismal water shouting, "Praise the Lord!" The folks in the church said they had never seen a more glorious look on anybody's face. Those chocolate eyes actually danced. I knew that he was the right man.

Brother Moore said he would be willing to marry us if we felt it was the Lord's leading. Both of us confirmed that this was God's perfect will for our lives. I was afraid the pastor would ask me about Mickey, but he never did mention him when Roger and I went to talk about getting married.

I had learned one lesson. I would not rush into setting a wedding date as I had back in the spring. "If a thing is worth having," I told Roger, "it's worth waiting for. Let's wait this one out and be sure it is God's plan for us."

Kim was attending St. Paul's Christian Academy where she was assigned a Bible lesson every day. Often I would help her at night before she went to sleep. Her lesson for the first week of November came from Genesis: the story of Joseph. Jackie Monaghan was spending the nights with me that week, and the two of us became interested in helping Kim with her Bible lesson on Joseph.

I was intrigued with the story. Joseph made his older brothers jealous by telling them his dreams of how they would one day bow down before him and by bragging about his coat of many colors—a special gift from his father. His brothers plotted to kill him but instead sold him to a slave dealer who took him down to Egypt. There he was assigned to a high ranking military officer, Potiphar, to work as his houseboy. Potiphar's wife was attracted to Joseph and tried to seduce him. Joseph refused her advances, however, saying that to sleep with her would be a "sin against God." Angry at being rejected, she told her husband Joseph had tried to rape her. Joseph was thrown into prison where he remained for a number of years. He was released only after Pharaoh had a series of prophetic dreams which he discovered Joseph could interpret. Impressed with Joseph's great ability, the Pharaoh made him second in command in Egypt. When famine sent his long-lost brothers down to Egypt to buy grain, Joseph recognized them, forgave them and set them up in a favored place in the nation. In the end, all that had been lost in the beginning was restored.

That night after Kim had gone to bed, Jackie and I stayed up talking about the story of Joseph. Naturally I was interested in his behavior around Potiphar's wife. I never remembered hearing that name before. Why had Joseph acted as he did? What was the secret of his integrity? He had an opportunity not only to satisfy himself with her but to better himself socially. And he refused both—saying he had to obey God. What did all that mean? How was it possible for him to know what God wanted?

The next morning I had an appointment at a nearby beauty shop. I was sitting down under the dryer when Jackie came in carrying a book. She had a funny look on her face.

"What is it?" I asked, motioning to the book.

"Well, I don't think you're going to believe this," she said. "A girl named Vicky down the hall—you've never met her—handed me this book. The minute I looked at it, I knew it was for you."

Jackie handed it to me. It's title: *The House of Potiphar.*

I felt a chill go down my spine. Things kept dropping into my life in mysterious ways. I sensed that in the pages of that book I would find the answers to my questions. All the more reason for being afraid to even open the book, much less to read it.

I dropped it into my purse and for some reason began carrying it with me, hoping, perhaps, that whatever message it contained would be transferred to me by osmosis. I read the first chapter, but I was afraid to go on. Everywhere I went, however, the book went with me. I suspected that sooner or later I would have to read it.

It was a Sunday afternoon in early November. The leaves

had finally dropped to the ground in front of our house on
Stonewall Jackson Court. Roger had spent Saturday afternoon helping Kim and me rake them into huge piles, then
he had gone with us to church Sunday morning. Wilma
Reid had fixed us all a big Sunday dinner. Afterwards we
enjoyed the view into the front yard through the French
doors which covered the entire front of the dining room.
We could see all the way to the top of the hill where the
tour buses, full of people who wanted to see the homes of
country music stars, turned around and started back down
the hill.

Kim started counting how many had come by. Most of
them were van-type buses, carrying eight to ten people. We
were the last house on the street, so the buses turned around
in the cul de sac and started back down right in front of
our place.

Then a light blue van pulled up in front of our house,
and the people got out with their cameras and started taking
pictues. They were just about to leave when Roger stood
up and pulled me by the hand. "Come on. Let's go out and
say hi to those folks. That'll give them a thrill."

This, coming from Roger, was a surprise. He had always
been a loner and could be unpleasant with people. He was
also highly protective of me and didn't like people hugging
and kissing me and seeking my autograph. Thus it was
totally out of character for Roger to stand up, right in the
middle of our dessert, and ask me to go out in the yard
and meet the people in the van.

"Sure," I beamed, "I'd love to do that."

The minute the folks at the van saw us coming through
the front door—Roger, Kim and me—they grabbed their
cameras again and came running across the yard. We met
them, chatted for a few moments, let them take our pictures
and signed autographs for all. It wasn't until later that we
discovered the van was not a regular tour bus; two families
from out of town had made a special trip by the house in
the van to take pictures.

Back at the dinner table we were drinking coffee and
finishing up Wilma's blueberry pie when we saw the van
return to the front of the house. A man came to the door.

Roger answered the doorbell and returned a few moments later with a business card in his hand.

"It was those folks again," he said. "They came back to tell us how much they appreciated the autographs. The man is a car dealer from Nebraska. He said if we were ever through there, he'd sure love for us to stop off and see them."

Nebraska? That's where Carolyn Abke, the wife of the Nazarene preacher who had been praying for me for so long, was from. I shuddered. I always shuddered when I knew God was doing something special in my life, even if I didn't know what it was. I knew, though, it was no coincidence those Nebraska folks had stopped by the house.

Ten days later I found in my mail an envelope from Nebraska. Inside was a letter and a photograph.

The writer was a Nazarene pastor. He said he and a member of their church, the automobile dealer, were the ones who stopped by our house that Sunday afternoon. He enclosed a copy of one of the pictures they had taken. It was a photo of Roger, Kim and me in front of our house. On the back he had written: "Jeannie C. Riley, her husband Roger and their daughter Kim. A fine Christian family."

I stood up in my upstairs bedroom for a long time, staring at that picture. Of course they had assumed Roger was my husband and the father of my little daughter Kim. I hadn't told them he was or wasn't my husband. I just introduced him as Roger. As I looked at that picture of the three of us, I thought of the numbers on my digital clock: Mickey, Kim and Jeannie. Roger just didn't fit into the picture. He was not part of that original package God had put together back in Anson, Texas. I was angry. Angry at Roger for being in my life when he didn't belong. Angry at myself for not having the courage to say to those precious people from Nebraska that he was not my husband.

I thought about Joseph who had the courage to say, when approached by the wife of Potiphar, "How can I do this thing and sin against God?" Yet I had gone right ahead and done it. I was walking in deception. I had deceived myself into believing all this was acceptable to God. Roger and I shared the "beautiful" things of life together—poetry, music and beautiful scenery. Mickey wasn't interested in things like that. He was a West Texas cowboy with blue jeans and grease under his fingernails. He worked at a greasy old service station and talked about cows and pigs. He had never asked me to sit in the den at night, sunk deep into a shag carpet, cuddling in front of a crackling fire while sandalwood and vanilla candles burned on special holders, listening to sad guitar music from a soft stereo and talking in whispers about things romantic. He didn't enjoy reading poetry to me while I had my head in his lap. He didn't love to stop the bus and walk with me through a flower-covered field, stand with his arms around me as we gazed at purple mountains in the distance or walk silently under a star-filled sky on a crisp autumn night. He didn't even pray with me—as Roger and I were beginning to do— or sit in church and hold my hand while listening to an eloquent preacher talk about the love of God. No, all he did was work, drink beer and tell me he would wait for me until I returned to the place where he felt I belonged, as his wife.

It didn't seem fair to have to give up such an interesting person as Roger and be cast into the prison cell of marriage to Mickey. Then I thought of Joseph. He had been in a prison before—that deep pit his brothers had put him in. He knew what it was like to be locked up and forgotten. But rather than go against the purpose of God, rather than disobey what he knew God wanted him to do, rather than compromise and become the kind of person who gave in to self-pleasure, he chose to run the risk of being thrown back into prison—a prison far worse than the one he came out of—just because God had spoken to him. It took some kind of faith to do that. Far more faith than I had. I knew, sooner or later, I was going to have to finish reading *The House of Potiphar.* Yet I was afraid—afraid to find out how the story actually ended.

Another week slid by. I was back on the road, carrying not only *The House of Potiphar* but that accusing picture with me. Every time I looked at it I wanted to cry.

Roger sensed something was wrong and pressed me for a Christmas wedding. Weak, confused, I said okay. I knew

I needed to make plans, but all I could do was cry.

Then came another letter from Nebraska: from Carolyn Abke in Sidney. I had written her once or twice and sent her a Christmas card the year before, but I had not heard from her since. Now it was the week before Thanksgiving 1974. She began her letter by telling me how many folks she had talked to who had heard me testify. She was writing to thank me for being faithful. Then she said:

> Praise the Lord. How happy we were to hear from you through some friends—fellow Nazarenes. We have just come from our district camp meeting, and some of our dearest friends told us they stopped by your house. How special it was that you and your husband came out to speak to them. I just can't praise the Lord enough. Remember how I wrote that I couldn't tell you that I had been praying for your salvation until I found out it had occurred; well, the same is true with your marriage. I have been praying since the moment of your salvation that your marriage would be restored. Now my dear friends tell me that you and your husband are back together. Isn't our God wonderful?

The letter sent daggers through my heart. My hands were trembling so badly I couldn't hold the sheet of paper steady enough to read.

There was a P.S. on the back. She wrote:

> Your testimony has meant so much to so many. Now that your marriage is healed, I believe God wants you to pass that gift of healing to others. There is a 15-year-old boy in our local hospital who is dying of cancer. We've all tried to witness to him, but somehow he has not been able to receive Jesus as his Lord. He's a great admirer of yours. If you will put your testimony on tape and send it to him, we're hopeful he will receive the Lord Jesus before he slips into eternity.

She had enclosed a blank cassette tape and a stamped, addressed envelope.

I dropped the tape as though it were filled with fire. Then I stared at it on the floor and began to cry. I felt as though

I held in my shaking hands the eternal fate of a dying boy—and I could do nothing about it. How could I? Hadn't I become one of the hypocrites I sang about in "Harper Valley PTA"? I knew Jesus was Lord. I knew He could save that boy. But there was no way I could pretend to be something I wasn't.

I dropped to my knees on the bedroom floor. "Oh, God, why are You doing this to me? Why don't You leave me alone? Don't You know I can't do any more? I have prayed. I have done everything. Why does this torment continue?"

"But have you done everything?" It was such a still, small voice that I almost missed it. It came from deep in my heart. Certainly no one else could have heard it, for I could barely distinguish it myself.

"Everything, Lord!" I cried out.

"If you love me, you will do as I say," He seemed to say gently.

There it was again. Love is something you do. But do what? I didn't have a smoking or drinking habit. I wasn't singing vulgar songs anymore. I had even dropped the bars and night clubs on my circuit. I was keeping all the commandments I knew to keep. I was going to church, even tithing my income. What more was necessary?

The story of the rich young ruler who came to Jesus asking what he needed to do to receive eternal life flashed through my mind. What was it Jesus had told him? "One thing thou lackest: go thy way, sell whatsoever thou hast, and give to the poor, and thou shalt have treasure in heaven: and come, take up the cross, and follow me" (Mark 10:21).

"What else do I have to get rid of, Lord?" I wept.

There was silence. I looked around the room in frustration, and there was that big picture of Roger on my wall.

Was God waiting on that final decision, not just to turn my back on Roger, but to submit myself to my original husband before He would let me have "treasure in heaven"? Was this what "selling all I had" meant to me?

I could not. I looked at the cassette tape on the floor. I had no testimony. If this dying boy was looking to me as an example of one following Jesus, he was looking in the wrong place.

I do not know what happened to that boy, but I know from that moment I entered into my own hell. I was to sing in Pittsburgh on the weekend before Thanksgiving. The very thought of going to that steel-smelting city terrified me. I was going through my own smelting process. I could not sleep. I could not eat. My body broke out in an angry rash, and there were dark circles under my eyes.

One night I locked myself in the bathroom and stretched out in a bathtub full of water. I imagined I was lying in my casket and in my mind let the people in my life pass by and look down at me. How did they feel? What did they think of me? There came Mama and Daddy. Wilma. Jackie. Roger. Helen and Gene and their children. Then came little Kim, her face swollen from crying. Finally there stood Mickey, looking down on me in the casket, my hands folded across my chest. He loved me most. I could see it in his face. His was the deepest grief. Why then, had I pushed him out of my life? Why was Roger there instead of the man who was my rightful husband?

I had never missed a concert before. No matter how I felt, I had always fulfilled my contract. There had been times when the boys in the band had to help me off stage before I fainted from weariness. There had been times when I had sung and didn't even realize I had sung. My lead guitar player used to joke that if they ever did put me in a coffin and someone came to the funeral waving an unfulfilled contract, I'd get up and sing.

But Pittsburgh? With those great furnaces? I was petrified.

The night before I was to leave, I opened my Bible to the place between the Old and New Testaments to read at random. My eyes fell on the last chapter of the last book of the Old Testament—Malachi 4. It began with terrifying words:

> "Watch now," the Lord of Hosts declares, "the day of judgment is coming, burning like a furnace. The proud and wicked will be burned up like straw; like a tree, they will be consumed—roots and all" (Malachi 4:1 TLB).

I was frightened. *Is this what you're doing to me, Lord?*

I asked silently, sitting crosslegged in my big bed with the Bible on my lap. *Are you going to burn me up?*

I could read no more. My eyes glanced backwards to the previous chapter on the opposite page:

> "But who can live when He appears? Who can endure His coming? For He is like a blazing fire refining precious metal and He can bleach the dirtiest garments! Like a refiner of silver He will sit and closely watch as the dross is burned away. He will purify the Levites, the ministers of God, refining them like gold or silver, so that they will do their work for God with pure hearts. Then once more the Lord will enjoy the offerings brought to Him by the people of Judah and Jerusalem, as he did before. At that time My punishments will be quick and certain; I will move swiftly against wicked men who trick the innocent, against adulterers, and liars, against all those who cheat their hired hands, or oppress widows and orphans, or defraud strangers, and do not fear me," says the Lord of Hosts. "For I am the Lord—I do not change. That is why you are not already utterly destroyed (for my mercy endures forever)" (Malachi 3:2-6 TLB).

I imagined God sitting in front of a crucible with a white-hot fire burning underneath. Inside was molten silver, bubbling. God was sitting patiently, waiting. How would He know when the molten silver was pure? When He could see His face in it? Why was He sitting? Because such a process takes a long time? But the promise remained. Having accepted Christ, I was now adopted into this family. Although I was the daughter of Oscar and Nora Stephenson, I was also a "son of Jacob." Therefore I would not be consumed in the fire—only purified.

I slept that night for the first time since Carolyn Abke's last letter. The next day I left for Pittsburgh. I knew the fires would not destroy me, but I sensed the day of reckoning was close at hand.

19

No Turning Back

There was a picture that hung on Grandma Moore's wall long after Grandpa had died. It was an artist's rendition titled "The Rapture." There was a couple working in the field. One was still hoeing cotton while the other was being carried up to heaven. In the background was a church. Some were standing around talking while others were being swept up into the clouds. As a child I used to stand and stare at the picture, wondering if I would be left when Jesus returned to call His own. The fear of being left behind had always haunted me.

Now that fear seemed greater than ever before.

The last day in Pittsburgh was one of the most difficult of my life. I had reread the first three chapters of *The House of Potiphar* but could go no further. The story of Joseph presented too high a standard. I just couldn't picture him as I was—huddled in a lonely hotel room, unable to make decisions, too miserable to even try to cope with life. I could see no way out of my situation other than to flee to West Texas. I spent that entire afternoon savoring the thought, bundled in my bed. I would run and hide from the people who were putting so much stress on my life. I would call Wilma, ask her to explain to Kim, and I would go back home to Anson, Texas. There I would crawl into my bed and snuggle up with my teddy bear.

Just before dinner Roger knocked on my door. He was rooming down the hall but somehow sensed I was going through deep torment. He had kept away from me all weekend except for the necessary business contacts.

"You might as well tell me what's bothering you," he said. "Everyone in the band knows something's wrong."

I was tempted to lie to him, just to see if he would get angry and disappear out of my life. Anything would have been easier than telling him the truth—that I was battling with God over my life. But how can a Jacob tell anyone he is wrestling with an angel? I was too engrossed in the fight. Yet I knew if I turned loose of my adversary, I would be lost.

"I can't tell you," I said truthfully. "I don't know why I am so miserable. But if I don't find some peace of mind, I'm going to go crazy."

Roger had nothing to offer. Even though he claimed to be a Christian, when it came to understanding spiritual struggles he was blank. I determined when I got back to Nashville I was going to make an appointment and talk with Brother Moore who had said over and over that I had to find my own way to God. "If I show you the way, then you will be dependent on me," he had said. "You must hear from God yourself."

I was relieved that he had not condemned me or tried to "straighten me out." But, on the other hand, it angered me that he would not tell me what was right or wrong—insisting I discover that for myself. At the same time, I didn't know anyone else to talk to, and I desperately needed some answers.

Back in Nashville, I went to Brother Moore's house one Wednesday afternoon. There in his living room I poured out my heart for almost four hours. I told him everything. I told him about my disappointments with Mickey. I told him of my hopes for Roger. I told him how I had prayed, asking God to give me a sign—Mickey or Roger—and how Roger had accepted the Lord. I told him of the conflict in my soul and pleaded with him to pray that God would show me a sign, a miraculous sign, because I was fixing to do something that might be the biggest thing I had ever done in my life—marry Roger.

He didn't say anything. He just sat and listened, offering a loving, listening ear. After I had talked myself out and was sitting back in the chair, my eyes swollen from crying and my hands shaking, he finally spoke.

"We're going to pray in just a minute. You may not get an immediate answer; on the other hand, God may speak to you clearly. The Lord might choose to perform just the miracle you're begging for. But I am confident of this: as badly as you want to know what is right for your life, the Lord will not let you down. He will show you something. If you want out of this misery as badly as you say you do, then He will show you the way—although it might be something much different from what you expect."

I was almost hoping he would advise me to leave Roger. But he was noncommittal in that area. "I cannot tell you what to do, Jeannie. Only the Lord knows the situation, and only He knows what is best for you in your circumstance. You're going to have to trust Him to shut the wrong doors and open the right ones. He will give you peace about this. Now, we're going to pray because His child is miserable and needs an answer."

So we knelt there in his living room. I kept my eyes open while he was praying, looking out the curtains, expecting to see a sign in the clouds. I had seen a star once, in the clear afternoon West Texas sky. Why not again? But there was nothing. He ended the prayer.

I was drained. Disappointed. I had done everything I knew to do, but still I could not resolve my feelings with what I knew I should do.

Brother Moore walked me to the door and then, in a final gesture, he reached out and put his hands on my shoulders. Looking me straight in the eye, he prayed: "God, restore to Jeannie the years the locusts and the cankerworm have eaten."

It was a strange saying. I suspected it was from the Bible. When I got home the first thing I did was go up to my bedroom, close the door and take down my King James Bible with the concordance. I looked up "cankerworm" and finally traced down the verse. It came from the book of Joel:

> That which the palmerworm hath left hath the locust
> eaten; and that which the locust hath left hath the
> cankerworm eaten; and that which the cankerworm
> hath left hath the caterpiller eaten (Joel 1:4).

It was the description of my life. But what was it Brother Moore had prayed? I looked on, eagerly, through the short book of Joel. In the second chapter I found the answer:

> Therefore also now, saith the Lord, Turn ye even to
> me with all your heart, and with fasting, and with
> weeping, and with mourning: And rend your heart,
> and not your garments, and turn unto the Lord your
> God: for He is gracious and merciful, slow to anger,
> and of great kindness, and repenteth him of the evil . . .
> And I will restore to you the years that the locust hath
> eaten, the cankerworm, and the caterpiller, and the
> palmerworm . . . (Joel 2:12-13, 25).

I prayed that night harder than I had ever prayed in all my life. If God did not act, I was lost.

The next day was Thanksgiving. Mickey came by the house early in the morning to tell Kim good-by. He was leaving with a friend to drive to Arkansas on a hunting trip. Kim and I were in the den watching Macy's parade on television. I watched as Kim jumped into Mickey's arms, and they sat together on the sofa, Mickey dressed in his hunting clothes, his leather jacket with the lamb's wool collar and old blue jeans, hugging Kim and talking silly to her—telling her he was going to bring her a big deer.

"I don't want a deer, Daddy," she said. "I want a pony."

Mickey laughed and looked over at me. "Well, one of these days you're sure gonna have that pony."

"Will it be on a farm, Daddy?"

"Yup, a great big farm with a big white farm house and pretty fences around the pasture."

"Goodie, Daddy, and you and Mama can live in the house and I'll ride the pony."

"Well, baby, you just keep on praying, and I'll bet the

good Lord will give you everything you want." He paused, and then in a soft voice said, "And while you're at it, pray for your old daddy, too. Okay? He sure needs it."

"I do, Daddy. I pray for you, for Mama and for the pony."

Mickey swatted her on the seat and laid his hand on my shoulder on the way out. "Take care of my baby," he said. "And take care of yourself, too."

"And you be careful, too," I said as he walked toward the door.

I wanted to say more. He was going hunting. With guns. I had prayed the Lord would give me a sure sign what I was to do, to take me out of my indecision. What if that meant something was going to happen to Mickey?

Suddenly I was out of my chair, running to catch Mickey before he got to the front door. I grabbed him and hugged him tightly.

"What's this all about?" he said, putting his arms clumsily around me because of his heavy jacket.

I just hung on. "I don't know," I said finally. "Just be careful. Please."

He stepped back and took my face in his hands. I was aware of how rough his hands were, his fingers calloused and cracked from working.

His fingers smelled of tobacco; there was grease under his nails. He held my face for a moment, looking deep into my eyes.

"You still care, don't you?" he said softly.

I nodded, my face between his weathered hands, tears in my eyes. I couldn't speak.

Slowly, deliberately, he reached down and kissed me on the mouth. It was a gentle, lingering kiss. I responded, pulling myself up to him, trying to draw myself all the way into him. Then, just for a moment, I relaxed in his arms. It felt good, secure, being there.

He held me for the moment, then dropped his arms. "I gotta go," he said, his voice the way it always had been. "My buddies won't wait too long. Take care, y'heah?" And he was out the door.

I leaned against the door, hugging myself and shivering.

Then Kim was at my skirt, asking me why I was crying. I took her hand. "Come on, little darling, let's go watch the parades on TV."

Mickey returned safely Friday afternoon. He stopped by the house. I ran to the front door and once more threw my arms around him. We stood just inside the door, talking.

"I just knew you'd be back safe," I laughed. "I found a verse of Scripture that says, 'The eyes of the Lord are in every place, beholding the evil and the good.' "

"Well, now," Mickey said, stepping back and giving me a silly grin through his mustache, "just what does that mean?"

"Oh," I said, embarrassed, "it doesn't mean God was out there peeking on you to see if you were doing anything bad. It means He was watching out for you—whether you were good or bad. That gave me a lot of comfort."

Mickey laughed. "Between you and God I ain't got a chance, do I?"

I patted his shoulder. "You smell like liquor and smoke," I said.

"And you love me anyway, don't you?" Mickey grinned.

I pulled back and sat down on the stairs. "I don't know, Mickey. But I'm praying God will give me an answer—this weekend."

Mickey wanted to take Kim home with him since he hadn't been with her on Thanksgiving Day. I consented. Roger and I had plans to go shopping on Saturday afternoon anyway. The stage was set if God was going to show me something. But I was braced against the disappointment. I had asked Him so many times in the past, and nothing had happened.

Roger was supposed to come by the house about noon. The house was empty. I paced the floor waiting. He had never been this late. He was living in the rooming house with a friend and didn't have a phone. I began to feel fidgety, but the stillness of the empty house seemed to settle like a soft blanket. That book, *The House of Potiphar,* kept reappearing in my thoughts, demanding, tormenting me to read it.

I walked upstairs to my big bedroom and sat on the side of the bed, holding the book in my hands. Where was Roger? Why didn't he show up? I hated the stillness, the quiet. For years I had done everything possible to surround myself with activity and noise. Now it was as if the whole world had suddenly stopped. I was alone in the house. Even the noise of the traffic outside was hushed. It was like that afternoon in the cemetery at Anson when the entire world came to a halt, and God had spoken to me from the star. Now it seemed to be happening again. If there was no noise, I would create my own.

I began to cry. Softly at first, then louder. The sound of my own weeping seemed to help. Then, suddenly, I was out of control. Tears flowed like waves on the cliffs, crashing, then pouring back to the sea. I hammered on the book with my fists. I got up and paced around the room. Then I sprawled on my stomach, my hands beating the floor as I opened up and let all the frustration, the pain, the guilt, the hurt pour out of my inner being.

How utterly wretched you are, I seemed to say to myself. *Look at you, wallowing like an animal, absolutely wallowing on the floor. If you were out in the yard, you would be rooting up the soil with your nose. You have become an animal. You, child of the King, are nothing more than a wretched, miserable dog. Look at you, created only a little lower than the angels; you, a princess, a daughter of the King—just look at you.*

The more I talked to myself, the louder I howled—long, anguished wails.

Suddenly I was aware of other sounds. My own weeping subsided as I stopped to listen. From somewhere outside the window there were echoes of my own howls. I crawled from my place on the carpet, which was now wet with tears, to the ledge of the window. Peering over the sill, I looked down on the front yard. There was a pack of dogs, the dogs of the neighborhood who had heard my wails and had gathered in the front yard. They were looking up at my window, howling and whining in sympathy.

I collapsed on the floor. Utterly wasted. I had become one of them. *You can go no lower,* I heard a quiet voice say within. *You're going to have to do something different from what you've been doing. You're going to have to let go, obey Me and trust Me.*

"Oh, God," I moaned out loud, "what do You want me to do?"

Once again there was stillness. The quiet again entered the room, and I rested, my eyes closed, my body relaxing. When I opened my eyes, I saw the book still on the floor near the end of the bed where I had dropped it. "Yes, Lord," I murmured, "I'll read it. I'll read it now."

I crawled across the floor to the book and picked it up. For long moments I sat on the carpet, looking at it. Then I stood up and headed downstairs to the living room—book in hand.

For the next three hours the phone didn't ring, there was no one at the door, not a sound in the house. I am normally a slow reader because of my weak eyes, but there in the living room with the big windows all around and the November sun pouring light into the house, I remained alone with the story of Joseph as related in *The House of Potiphar.*

It was as though I was there—in Egypt with Joseph. I lived through his prison experiences. I, too, had been in prison; only with me it was a prison of my own making, a prison of self-devices. I realized that my career had been "bound" as surely as if I were in chains. Others had bound me. My image. Shelby Singleton. Even "Harper Valley PTA." What I thought had set me free had actually put me in bondage. I lived through Joseph's lean years and then the years of fatness. I was with him when his brothers came down to Egypt to buy grain. I wept as he identified himself to them and forgave them and later as he put his arms around his old daddy, Jacob, who had thought him dead only to find him alive and prospering under the blessing of God. Oh, how I wanted that, too.

I was crying so hard I could barely see the pages. "I want you to go back to your family," I heard the Lord whisper. "I will restore it just the way it was, only better."

I slipped out of that gold-colored easy chair. So symbolic, I thought. Sitting in a gold-colored chair and missing the blessings of God. What the world thought was my mountain top was actually the dark valley of materialism. I had been to the top of the charts, only to find the top was really bottom. What was it Jesus had said about the first being last and the last first? Now God was saying He wanted to restore all I had left behind in my striving to be number one.

My heart was pounding as I turned to the last page in the book, reading as I knelt on the floor. Each word seemed to leap off the page at me, and then I reached the last line: "I shall restore to thee the years the locusts and the cankerworm have eaten."

It was the exact wording of Brother Moore's prayer. Kneeling there on the carpet I felt a surge of power course through my body, short-circuiting my nervous and muscular systems until I went limp before God—flat on my face on the carpet. I was not unconscious. I was more alive than I had ever been. But my body was as if it were dead, and I had been resurrected into the throne room of God Himself. I could hear myself laughing, then crying, then laughing again. "Yes, Lord, yes," I said over and over. Then, "Oh, I'm free. The Spirit has set me free from my prison."

I slowly regained my natural senses and sat up. My watch said 3:30 p.m. I had been reading for more than three hours. Now I knew what I had to do.

Shortly thereafter I drove up in the driveway in front of Roger's apartment. I honked my horn. He came out the door, pulling on his leather jacket as though I was just on time and had come to pick him up to go shopping. When I rolled down the window on my side of the car, he came over to talk to me.

Then he saw my face and stepped back. It was as though he could tell by looking at me that something unusual had happened. My heart faltered, but I knew there was but one way I could go.

"Roger, I just came to tell you: I've had my reckoning with the Lord. I must do what He has told me to do."

He stepped up to the open car window then, stood half bent over, looking at me. His eyes were wide, his face expressionless.

"He has told me what He wants me to do," I said deliberately, "and I'm going to do it. He's told me if I do what He tells me to do, He will make my life more abundant than ever before. I'm going to follow Him. I'm going back to Mickey."

He straightened up, never taking his eyes off my face.

"I can't promise you anything better than that," he said. He turned and walked back into the house.

I rolled up the window, backed out into the street and drove away. It was not until I got to the end of the block that I realized what I had done. But I knew there was no looking back. What was it Kim had sung around the house?

> The cross before you,
> The world behind you,
> No turning back, no turning back.

I drove straight to Mickey's apartment. Kim was there, and I just knew it was the beginning of a brand new life.

The front door of the apartment building was unlocked. The sun was just setting in the west, casting a rosy reflection on the front of the porch. I paused, then walked into Mickey's front room without knocking. It was as if I were home.

Mickey was sitting in the black leather recliner chair in the living room, the chair Kim and I had given him for Christmas the year before. He and Kim were watching a football game on TV. I don't know what I expected him to do, maybe for him to fall on his knees before me, maybe weep and hug my neck in thanksgiving. But when I looked at him, he was the most unattractive thing I had ever seen. He was unshaven and still had on his old dirty hunting clothes from the hunting trip. He had a beer in one hand and a cigarette in the other. It made no difference, I thought. There was no way to back out now.

I knelt beside his chair. He turned and looked through bleary eyes. "What's wrong with you?" he slurred.

I swallowed deeply. I knew what the Lord was requiring of me, and I was determined to do it. "I've just been talking with the Lord," I said nervously. "I think He wants us to serve Him together." Even as I said it I knew I was still trying to control things. Why couldn't I have just said, "I'm home," and left it there?

Mickey gave me a long look through bloodshot eyes. Slowly he took a swig from his can of beer. Part of the contents dribbled through the stubble of beard on his chin and dripped on his dirty shirt.

"Oh, yeah?" he said. "Well, He ain't told me that." He turned and resumed watching TV—leaving me on my knees, feeling like a fool as all the lights on my mountain top blinked out, leaving me in utter darkness.

20

Love Is Something You Do

I picked up Kim and drove home, leaving Mickey still in the chair, drinking beer and staring with bleary eyes at the TV.

It's too much, God, this thing You are asking of me.

I remembered Daddy's voice echoing across the years from that dismal night in the house. "It ain't a feeling. It's just doing."

It seemed as though God was adding a postscript, asking softly, *Are you willing to walk through the tough times, too?*

The next five days were days of constant testing. Roger was packing to return to New Hampshire. A lot of his stuff was at my house, so he was in and out. Every time I saw him I was tempted to go back on my decision. I bought him a beautiful Bible and inscribed it sentimentally, "This is for you, my love. I am putting you in God's hands." I gave him back his pictures. He wanted one of my miniskirt-and-boots outfits so he could remember what I looked like when he played behind me on stage. I gave it to him. The day he left I asked him to step into Wilma's room in my house while his friends packed the last of his belongings in a U-Haul truck Mickey had given him free of charge from his service station.

We knelt by her bed and, even though my heart was breaking, I prayed. When we stood, he had tears in his eyes.

"I'm leaving you with a prayer," I said. He nodded. He understood. But when he walked out, I knew I was free, regardless of what took place between Mickey and me.

And free I was. The next morning I awoke with songs running through my head. I grabbed a pencil and began writing down the words. It was the first time in years I felt like composing. Throughout the day—in fact, for the next month—I was overflowing with new music. The creative part of me, so long stifled, was suddenly opened. Like a mountain spring that had been clogged with dead leaves, I was suddenly clean and productive. I would awaken in the middle of the night with lyrics and melody, all intact, flowing from me. I would grab a pen and a tape recorder and quickly record the music before it disappeared back into my subconscious. Some of those songs have become the best songs I've ever done in my concerts.

Then Mickey called. He was going back to Texas for Christmas and wanted to take Kim with him. Did I mind?

"How would you like to take us both?" I blurted out.

There was silence on the other end of the phone. Then he replied, "You're kidding."

"No, I just wondered if you'd like to have us both along."

"You know I would," he said seriously.

"Well, plan on me, too, then," I said. "It will be good to see your folks again."

All the way out to Texas Mickey and I talked. I was writing songs as fast as I could, and he was sitting behind the steering wheel rattling on about anything that came to mind. We had a glorious time. Mickey's parents, Haskell and Lottie Riley, had moved to San Angelo, and they welcomed me back like I had just been off on a trip—though it had been four years since I had been in their house. His sisters, Pat and Lou, and their families acted as though I had never been gone. Even the children who had grown up in my absence, still called me Aunt Jeannie. Not a word was said about our divorce. I was just totally accepted. The healing had begun.

We arrived back in Nashville on December 28. I had come down with the flu and went directly to bed. I was supposed to fly up to Akron, Ohio, for a New Year's Eve concert at Rex Humbard's Cathedral of Tomorrow, but I didn't see how I could make it. I was so sick, it looked like I was finally going to have to cancel an engagement.

Even though my voice sounded like a bullfrog, the music director at the Cathedral, Danny Koker, insisted I should come on. Jackie, who had called him, had no success convincing him otherwise. I finally had to get on the phone with him.

"If you did come, what key would you do most of your songs in?" Koker pressured.

"You don't seem to understand." I croaked. "I can't sing. I can barely talk. There's no need to know my keys."

"I've talked with Rex Humbard," Koker continued as if he hadn't heard me. "We feel the Lord has arranged this time and insist you come on, regardless of the shape of your voice."

"But I can't . . ."

"I'm sure you can," he said back. "Why don't you sing one or two of your songs over the phone, and I'll know what key you're in and we'll get our orchestra . . ."

"I know I'll probably miss a blessing, but there's no way," I apologized.

I hung up and sat there shaking my head. That afternoon he called back. "The Lord wants you here," he insisted. "The devil is trying to rob you of a blessing. The same thing happened to Connie Smith the first time she was to sing at the Cathedral of Tomorrow. She got the victory over it, though, and you are going to get it also."

That was early afternoon on December 30. That evening I got another call from Danny Koker. He was at the Nashville airport. He had flown over from Akron and was on his way out to my house in a rented car.

"That's the most persistent man I've ever heard of," Wilma Reid said.

"Well, you might as well let him in when he gets here," I croaked. "Any man who comes that far must have something heavy on his mind."

Danny arrived at the house a little before 9:30 p.m. Wilma brought him up to my bedroom where I was tucked in with a vaporizer and a table full of cough medicine. He walked in and came straight to the side of the bed where he knelt down and began to pray, reaching over and putting his hand on my forehead while he did. When he finished, he explained that he was certain God had healed me and that I'd be in Akron the next night for the New Year's Eve service. I still felt just as sick as ever, but his faith was contagious. I gave him a couple of my tapes so he could get my keys for their orchestra at the Cathedral. He left to return to Akron.

The next day my fever broke. Although I was still hoarse, my voice was stronger. I called Mickey, and he agreed to fly to Akron with me. He, too, was impressed with what had happened the night before.

The huge Cathedral of Tomorrow was packed for the New Year's Eve service. It was a grand affair with a full orchestra on stage. Rex Humbard and the Humbard Family Singers were all there, dressed in formal clothes, leading the service. I'm a "fast fader" when it comes to singing. By that I mean that if I sing a lot early in the day, by night my voice becomes hoarse and husky. I had been protecting my voice, had barely spoken to Mickey on the plane and had not joined in the praise and worship songs the congregation had sung. At 10:30 p.m. Rex Humbard welcomed me, and I came to the stage. Mickey remained in his seat in the last row of the big auditorium, far back under the balcony.

I was surprised how strong my voice was, and as Danny had said, it grew stronger the more I sang. As midnight approached, I began to tell the congregation about my divorce and then my conversion experience. "Mickey Riley, my ex-husband, is here with me tonight," I said. Then I began to cry. I turned to the orchestra to sing "The Baptism of Jesse Taylor" when Rex Humbard stepped up and interrupted me.

"It's almost midnight," he said, putting his arm around my shoulders and turning to the crowd. "I want Jeannie to continue, but here at the Cathedral we love to pray for our guests at the beginning of the new year. Tonight, as the clock rings in 1975, I believe God wants to bless her with years of abundance."

There was that phrase again. There were to be seven years of spiritual blessing to follow these seven years of spiritual famine.

"I want all you people to stand," Rex said, "and stretch your hands toward Jeannie. Her ex-husband is in the congregation tonight, and since she has just mentioned him, I want him to come forward. At the stroke of the new year I want the two of them to kneel to receive this blessing. Mickey Riley! Come up here, please."

Everyone waited. I peered through the spotlights to where I knew Mickey was sitting. His seat looked empty. Then I saw him, hunkered down in the seat, his head pulled down into his shoulders like a turtle trying to slip into his shell. The folks around him didn't know who he was, but Rex Humbard kept saying, "Mickey Riley, where are you? Come on up here on the platform."

Still Mickey didn't move.

Rex turned to me. "Is he out there?" he asked.

"Yes, sir," I grinned. "He's back there on the back row, but he won't come forward."

"Guess I'll just have to go get him," Rex said, and he started off the stage and down the aisle toward Mickey's seat.

Mickey saw him coming and reluctantly stood up. The people began to applaud. They all stood to their feet while Mickey and Rex came back up on the platform. Mickey took my hand. I could feel his entire body shaking. The TV cameras were rolling, and everyone was standing with their hands stretched out toward us. And over it all was that huge lighted cross in the ceiling of the Cathedral.

Suddenly we were on our knees. I don't know if Mickey's legs just gave way from fright or whether we both, at the same time, realized we should be kneeling. Whatever, we found ourselves kneeling in the middle of that big stage, and Rex Humbard was standing in front of us with his hands on our heads. The room was suddenly filled with the sound of prayer. Five thousand people all praying. Rex and his wife, Maud Aimee, were praying. I was praying. The only one I could hear was Rex, and he was praying that God would "bless Mickey and Jeannie."

Leaving, I knew something good was about to happen. That prayer had been answered.

We flew back to Nashville after the service, arriving just before dawn. On the plane, before we landed, Mickey reached over and took my hand. "We might as well go ahead with it," he said.

I had my seat reclined and was resting.

"What'd you say?" I mumbled, half asleep.

"Too much has happened for it to be just coincidence," he continued. "We need to put both our eggs in one basket. It's time for us to get married again."

I turned toward him, snuggling up against his arm. "I know it sounds crazy," I said, "but even with everything that's gone on, I've never really been unmarried to you. Let's set a date and make it right."

As we stepped off the plane in Nashville and walked out to the parking lot to get the car, the sun was just coming up in the east. It was January 1. The cars in the parking lot were covered with a soft blanket of new snow. I took Mickey's arm with both my hands, holding to him as we made our way through the brisk air. I was alive. The years the locusts and cankerworm had eaten were being restored.

I asked Brother Moore to marry us at The Lord's Chapel. We set the date for January 26. Early in the month I caught a plane for Nevada where I had a three-day engagement at the Sahara-Tahoe at Lake Tahoe. Mickey drove me to the plane and kissed me good-by. I felt like a little girl, planning her wedding. Everyone seemed excited and happy.

I'm afraid the folks at the Sahara-Tahoe got more than they planned for. I put on my act, sang my songs and told the people what was happening in my life. It was a strange place to do it, with folks sitting there with drinks in their hands and the gambling tables and slot machines running full in the background, but I was too excited to hold it back.

A strange thing happened. As I shared in between songs,

telling the folks about my conversion to Christ, the huge gambling casino grew quiet. It was the same kind of stillness that descended that day in the cemetery in West Texas, the same quiet that filled the house the day I was immersed in reading *The House of Potiphar*—now, here it was that night in the Sahara at Lake Tahoe. All the background noise seemed to fade as I talked—the clink of glasses, the laughing and noise—it all stopped. Every eye was fixed on me as the Harper Valley PTA girl told how the only thing that had meaning to her now was Jesus Christ and His love.

The second night the same thing happened all over again. During the intermission, as I was backstage resting before my second act, a stage hand gave me a note. It was from a preacher in a nearby church. He said someone had called him and told him about my testimony the night before. He had gathered up about 20 of his flock, and they were all out there in the audience. Sure enough, when I went back on stage, I saw them. They stuck out like sheep in a goat pen, sitting back there at the tables, smiling and nodding as I talked and sang. It was a thrill to know I was being supported by my brothers and sisters in the kingdom even though we'd never met.

Mickey had sent me a dozen red roses for opening night, and I talked to him each evening on the phone. Over and over he told me how much he missed me and how much he loved me. He said he could hardly wait to meet me at the plane.

On the flight from Reno to Nashville, I felt like Cinderella returning to claim her glass slipper. Just before the plane landed in Nashville, I went back to the restroom and did a little primping. I wanted to have my hair combed just right, have just the right kind of perfume on my neck and wrists, so that when Mickey met me at the gate in the airport I would be just perfect.

I bounced off the plane and looked for Mickey. I didn't spot him at first, then I saw him staggering down the concourse toward me. He was dressed in his greasy old Exxon uniform and had so much alcohol in him it was a wonder his breath didn't ignite the airport. I wanted to run, but I stood still as he lumbered up to me, his scraggly beard sandpapering my face, his breath knocking me over, his greasy hands patting me on the back as he hugged me. He was drunk.

I was crushed. *Is he already taking me for granted? Is this what I am to put up with the rest of my life?*

I pulled loose from him and headed for the baggage claim area which opens onto the parking lot. All the way through the airport I walked three steps in front of him. He had left his car at my house and was driving my Cadillac. He brought the car around to the baggage area and I got in, Bible under my arm. Angry. Hurt. Had we come this far, only to come to this?

He tried to explain in his slurred voice. He had gotten off from work early so he could take his Levis suit by the cleaners to have it pressed before leaving for the airport. He wanted to look his best when I arrived, he said. But the cleaners couldn't do it right then, so he stopped by a pool room next door to wait. He began drinking with some of his friends, and by the time he remembered to get his suit, the cleaners had closed and he was staggering. He wasn't so wiped out he couldn't drive, but he was pretty shaky.

He apologized. Yet he was proud. When he saw I was just sitting stiffly in the car, my Bible on my lap, looking straight ahead, he sighed.

"It's no use, Jeannie," he mumbled. "I know I've let you down. I guess we just better call the whole thing off."

I felt the tears running down my face, but I just didn't see how I could give in to something like this.

"I guess you're right," I said softly, still staring through the windshield as we approached Mickey's apartment. "We can't go on like this. I thought God wanted us to serve Him together, but I don't see how . . ."

"I'll just get out at my apartment," Mickey said. "You can take the car on home. Wilma has fixed us a big meal over at your house, and I thought we'd celebrate together. But I guess I've messed it up for good, haven't I?"

"I guess you have," I said. "You've already done your celebrating. I need to go on home and try to figure out what I'm going to do."

I let him out at his apartment and didn't even wait to see if he could stagger up the front walk to the door. I drove away, complaining bitterly to the Lord. Instead of taking the short cut to my house, I drove along the main roads. I needed time to think. And pray.

I just can't believe he's done this, Lord, I cried, *after all we've been through . . .*

You thought all you had to do was crook your finger and he'd come running, is that it? I recognized that still, quiet voice in my heart.

But, Lord, I thought You told me we were to serve You together?

Your idea of serving me may not be exactly what I had in mind, the gentle voice whispered in the quiet place of my heart. *Maybe I had something much different in mind. I don't need your service as much as I need you. I have thousands of people who are serving me. I want you to obey me.*

I pulled up to the stop sign at Leland Lane. Ordinarily I would have gone straight on up toward my street. But for some reason the car didn't seem to want to go. I sat there for a moment, my foot on the brake.

You took him for better or worse. The voice had a smile in it. *And tonight sure is worse, isn't it?*

It isn't fair, Lord. Why do I have to do all the giving?

He is your husband, and if you are going to obey me, you will go back and submit to him.

No, I can't. Not like this. Not like he is. He's just a drunken klutz.

I tried to pull across the intersection, but the wheel was actually turning in my hand, forcing me to go back down the side street toward Mickey's apartment.

You said for better or worse. The voice was determined. It came over and over again: *For better or worse . . . for better or worse . . . for better or worse . . .*

Then I parked in front of Mickey's apartment. *Please, Lord!* I begged. Then the words to Kim's little song rang in my head again:

I have decided to follow Jesus,
No turning back, no turning back.

I left the car and walked into Mickey's apartment. The front door was ajar. I closed it gently behind me. Crossing the living room, I stood in the door to Mickey's bedroom. He was already in bed, clad only in his undershorts, smoking a cigarette. His eyes were bleary, and there was a long ash on the end of his cigarette. He looked up at me, his bearded face expressionless, his hair hanging into his eyes. He took a long draw on the cigarette. The ash fell down on the sheet and scattered on the side of the bed.

"What're you doin' back here?" he moaned.

"You're my husband. You always have been," I said quietly.

Stepping into the bathroom, I removed everything—my clothes, my self-will, my desire to control. Unconditional submission was what God wanted. I was weeping as I stepped back into the bedroom.

"This is where I belong," I said softly.

We talked long into the night, making our wedding plans. Even that seemed strange. For I felt we had always been married. But there were always the legalities. During those four years away from Mickey I had grown independent. God wanted me free, but He wanted me submitted to my husband. In my independence I believed I could return to Mickey, not so much as a wife, but as a spiritual boss, declaring, "We're going to serve God together." All that primping on the plane, walking in front of him through the airport—it was all my subtle way of maintaining control. It would have never worked. Mickey would have wound up being Mr. Jeannie C. Riley again. Instead, God wanted me to return in humility, submit myself to him despite the unattractive circumstances and say, "Here I am, Mr. Drunk, ready to become Mrs. Drunk if that is what God wants."

That's not what God intended, however. He had something much better in mind for me than to be Mrs. Drunk—just like he had something much better than for Mickey to become Mr. Jeannie C. Riley. He wanted to restore us in proper, divine order. He wanted to give Mickey a new, husbandly authority. And He wanted me to be willing to submit to Mickey's wise counsel and loving protection—which became evident almost instantly the minute I came down off my throne and allowed God to place my husband on the throne of our home.

We went through the wedding ceremony three weeks later, January 26, 1975, at The Lord's Chapel—12 years from the day we said our first vows in Anson. It was a simple wedding in that simple building. No carpet on the floor. No padded pews. Just hard metal folding chairs. Mickey wore his denim suit, the one he had left at the cleaners, complete with cowboy boots. His hair was slicked back in a shoulder-length pompadour and his mustache trimmed and waxed with the ends turned up in cute little handlebars. He was handsome! I dressed in an old-fashioned dress, off-white with tiny pink flowers and a high collar, with an antique brooch at the throat. I was no longer the Harper Valley PTA girl; I was Jeannie C. Riley-Riley.

All Mickey's friends—his old drinking buddies—were there. The big burly Wilson brothers wiped away tears. Kinda-Mama and Royce were in the back, rejoicing. Even Shelby sat there grinning.

Behold, all things are become new.

Connie Smith, great with child, sang "The Wedding Prayer." The organ played Grandpa Moore's favorite hymn, "Amazing Grace," as we came down the aisle. Gene was best man, and Helen was my matron of honor. Kim, nine years old and so proud she was ready to pop, stood between us at the altar as our flower girl. Her prayers had been answered.

Mickey made the honeymoon trip a surprise. "Remember how I used to call you up in the middle of the night and tell you we could have breakfast in Acapulco, Mexico? And how you always refused? Well, this time you can't say no. Tomorrow morning you're going to wake up and have breakfast in bed—with me in Acapulco."

21

Mickey, Kim and Me

There are still a lot of unanswered questions about my life. Why was I so compulsive? Why was I so wishy-washy? Why, when given the opportunity to choose between right and wrong, didn't I always choose the right?

I still do not understand why I was so insecure, why I was so gullible. I didn't like myself. All those suggestive poses for pictures, the saucy looks, the brash behavior—it was all an act to keep folks from knowing the real me. I was so afraid I would be unloved—even by God—if I got honest.

When I finally surrendered to God, He promised me seven years of abundance to match the seven years of famine I had just been through. That promise has been fulfilled. I can hardly believe how easy it is to love everyone—even myself. Yet, even during the times of blessing there have been times of doubt, fear and questions. At the same time, however, there has always been the underlying knowledge that God controlled my life— and my destiny.

Three weeks after we returned from our honeymoon, I received a tape from Roger. I was reluctant to listen to it. But Roger had included a note that said, "Please listen to this alone. If you feel you need to share it with anyone else, including Mickey, go ahead. But at least listen privately first."

On the tape Roger said he had been reading the Bible and discovered that in order to be in a right relationship with God, he needed to make restitution to those he had hurt.

"I know I've hurt you more than any other person in the world," he said. "That's the reason I ask you to forgive me."

On the rest of the tape he took time to go back over every event he could remember where he had cheated me—or cheated on me. He reminded me of an instance when I had stopped by his apartment after a prayer meeting. I had found him with another woman. He had lied and said she was a friend of his roommate. Actually she was the stripper from the Red Lion. He confessed squandering his money and borrowing from the road money, doubting that he could ever pay it back.

As I listened, I realized I had never known the real Roger. All I had known was the image he had held up before me. Now that he was getting honest, I realized I had loved someone who wasn't. Now that I saw him as he really had been, I discovered I had been in love with an image—not a man.

However, my relationship with Mickey, with whom I shared the tape, had never been that way. I had known Mickey from childhood. He had never hidden anything from me—good or bad. Although I had constantly looked for some knight in shining armor to carry me away on a white horse to some romantic hideaway, in actuality there were no such knights. Only images. Mickey alone, among my acquaintances, was real.

With Roger, as with all the other men who had paraded through my life behind masks, I had loved the mask but never known the man. His tape helped clear the memories. It was the Lord's way of setting me free—free so there is nobody from my past who now has a claim on me.

It's just Mickey, Kim, me—and God.

Shortly after Mickey and I were remarried, he found the farm that Kim had been praying for—complete with pony. The farm was outside the little community of Franklin, Tennessee, just a few miles from downtown Nashville. It included 200 acres of rolling pasture and woods, a huge stable, several smaller buildings and a big old antebellum house with white columns.

One afternoon, during our move to the farm from the house on Stonewall Jackson Court, Mickey found the note I had written before I left for Germany, almost three years before.

"That's not fair," I pouted as he sat on the floor and opened the envelope. "I told you not to open that unless I died."

He grinned and pulled the letter out of the wrinkled envelope. "Now I'm gonna find out what you really thought of me," he said. He read the note out loud:

> Today I saw the sun through the windows of my heart and the light was you. I know now that I never stopped loving you. I was just lost. Thank you with all my heart for the other light of my world—Kim Michelle. Please raise her to be a Christian.

Mickey's voice broke, but he read on.

> I pray to God that you'll believe me when I say I love you. I now realize you are the one and only love of my life. I'm just waiting for God . . .

He could read no farther. I laughed nervously, but his face was serious. "You really did love me, didn't you?" he said.

I nodded. "I thought you knew," I said.

Sometime back before we had separated, there had been an afternoon at the house when Mickey, Kim and I were together. Kim was about four years old, maybe five. A fierce thunderstorm had come up, and the big plate glass sliding doors in the den were vibrating as the lightning smashed to the ground near the house, and the thunder rolled across the city.

Kim ran to her daddy. "Daddy, I'm scared!" she wailed.

"Don't worry, honey," Mickey joked, patting her head. "That's just God's way of showing He's angry with us."

Kim stood for a moment, staring wide-eyed at her daddy. Then she ran quickly to the sliding glass doors. Peering up into the sky, she yelled, "I love you, God! I love you!"

Time and again, across the years, I have remembered that little scene. How sincere she was. How easy it was for her to say it.

I, too, had loved like that. Deep in my heart I had loved God and loved Mickey. But it took the lightning flashes to bring it out.

There are still a lot of loose ends in my life. Even though I've moved from Harper Valley to the mountain top, there are still times of doubt, depression—even defeat. Mickey is still not everything I would like him to be but he's my husband—and I love him too much to try to change him. God will have to do that.

At the same time, I'm not everything he wishes I was. I'm still compulsive. I get discouraged easily. But he knows Jesus Christ is my Lord, and he is my greatest fan.

On the road between our farm and Franklin there is a signboard that reads: "The family that prays together, stays together." Mickey saw that one day and remarked, "That's good. But it ought to read: 'The family that *stays* together—stays together.'"

We've done that. Even though I enjoy traveling on our bus across the nation—singing and sharing—I seldom take a trip without Mickey. And usually Kim is along, too.

I went through a period when I was uncomfortable with the song, "Harper Valley PTA." Now I realize that while it was God's way of bringing me to Him, it is also His sermon to me. Every time I sing it, even after all these years, I flinch as the sting of my own hypocrisy is brought to mind. Not only was I Mrs. Johnson with her miniskirt, but I was philandering Bobby Taylor. I was the widow Jones with her window shades up, I was Shirley Thompson with the nip of gin on her breath. No one was as big a hypocrite as I was. But now, praise God, things are different.

Since I submitted to Jesus Christ, and to my husband, I've discovered a new set of standards. They may not fit everyone else, but they fit me. And I will not back away.

An agent said to me recently, "I'm concerned about you, Jeannie. You're not the same girl you used to be. I know you've had some kind of religious experience, but you don't have to lie down and die just because you've become a Christian."

He was comparing me with other country singers who have become superstars. "Now all the folks talk about is Dolly Parton," he said seriously.

"Well, why not?" I said. "She's just about the prettiest thing ever to hit Nashville. You don't have to talk to me about Dolly. I've promoted her as much as I have myself. She's done great, and she'll do greater. But she's Dolly and I'm Jeannie. I don't have to be like her or anyone else."

He didn't understand. "Don't you want to get back to the top?"

I wanted to tell him about Jesus, how He had changed my life, but somehow I didn't think he'd understand. Maybe it was better just to let him see how my life had changed. That would at least start him to thinking.

"A lot of Nashville stars are religious," he argued. "But they keep their convictions to themselves."

My mind flashed back to Grandpa Moore, preaching on the street corner in Anson on a Saturday afternoon. Only a few old folks would gather to listen. Most just sneered— or laughed, and called him "Mad Dog Moore."

I guess I've gone full circle, because I've returned to the faith—and stability—of my old, street-preaching, Nazarene Grandpa. The world may one day call me "Mad Dog" too. That's the risk I'll have to run, I guess. But the prodigal daughter has returned to her Father's house.

Please don't misunderstand me. Of course I want to be successful. I'd love to be number one again. Now, more than ever, I have something to give the people—spiritually as well as musically. In fact, I enjoy performing more now than I ever have. At last I'm free to like myself—and to love others in a way I never could. It is God who has given me a love for those who hear me sing—instead of separating me from them as I once feared.

Yet I know success is more than being a top moneymaker. For me success must include peace of mind. And right now I'm content being a good wife and mother, singing in family shows around the country, composing some songs, cutting a few records and waiting before God.

I like to sing country songs. That's where my heart is, feeling the excitement of the crowd, responding to it. But the best times are in the afterglow of the county fairs and rodeos, as the lights go out, and I get to mingle with the people.

I remember singing at the Silver Spurs Rodeo in Kissimmee, Florida, one hot, humid, July night. It was a typical rodeo. There had been prancing horses with beautiful girls astride them; cowboys racing around the track at breakneck speed, swinging a rope and chasing calves; old men with weathered faces and sweat-stained hats who hugged their saddles like they had been born in them; cowboys tossed through the air off wildly bucking broncos, and steer-riding fools who hit the ground and rolled to keep from being stomped to death. Everyone was wearing boots, cowboy hats and dirty jeans. Everyone smelled a little bit like horse. And why not? Central Florida is cowboy country.

After it was all over, they pulled a stage out in front of the stands, set up the mikes and turned on the spotlights. My band kicked off the opening number and the crowd came alive again, this time clapping in unison as the spotlight picked me up walking across the rodeo track dressed in a white cowboy suit decorated with sequins and wearing a big white cowboy hat.

Someone handed me a mike, and I began belting out good old country music. I watched their faces as I sang, young faces of cowboys and cowgirls, weathered faces, faces with crinkles around the eyes, tough, leathery faces. They clapped their hands and stomped their feet. I shifted from country to gospel. In between songs I had a chance to tell them a little bit about my life, how fame had been my downfall, how I'd lost my husband and almost lost my mind. I sang a little more and then in a few words told them what Jesus had done for me. The crowd grew quiet. Even the toughest cowboys were listening.

Just because a man can rope and tie a calf in 10 seconds or can stay on the back of a bucking steer, does not mean he doesn't have empty spots in his life. So I sang and talked to those empty spots.

Then the band hit the familiar "dwoang, dwoang" introduction and, as I had done 10,000 times before, I was into Tom T. Hall's song about the meeting of the Harper Valley PTA.

It used to bother me that no matter what else I sang, that was the song they all seemed to be waiting to hear. But I've walked out of that valley now, and I'm on the mountain top—and it doesn't bother me anymore. I praise God for the song and for the message.

After the performance I grabbed a drink of water and as the lights in the big arena dimmed, walked toward the chute where the broncos came out. As I neared the fence, I saw a young, muscular cowboy standing shyly to one side.

"Miss Jeannie," he said, "can I talk to you?"

I walked over to him, and he reached out to shake my hand. "That was mighty purty," he said.

He was standing, one foot on the bottom rail of the rough wooden fence. Then he dropped his head. "Miss Jeannie . . ." he started again. He quickly reached into his pocket and pulled out a red bandana. Turning his head to one side, he spit his plug of chewing tobacco into the handkerchief and stuffed it into his pocket. Clearing his throat, he started again.

"Miss Jeannie, you said you'n your old man had some troubles. You got a divorce, didn't you?"

"That's right," I said. "But Jesus took care of that. We're back together. In fact, my husband's over there with the boys now, helping gather up the stuff."

He was fumbling for words. I waited. "Me'n my wife, we've only been married a year. Tomorrow's our anniversary, and she's up and left me. I . . ." And big tears sprang from his eyes and rolled down his tanned face.

He was no more than 20 years old. Blond, curly hair stuck up from under his hat. His little blond mustache was barely visible beneath the coat of dust he had picked up after the steer-roping contest.

"'Scuse me, ma'am . . ." he stammered, embarrassed over his tears. "I didn't mean to do all this. I just wondered if you'd say a little prayer for me sometime." Tears were washing little streaks down his dirty face.

Everything else faded into the night as I reached across

the fence and laid my hand on his arm. He quickly grabbed my fingers in his calloused hand, clutching me tightly. Again, it was like that afternoon in the cemetery in Anson when all the world stopped while God spoke to me. The milling crowds disappeared. The sounds of the animals snorting and thrashing in the stalls melted away. The noise of the cars and trucks with their horse trailers pulling out of the driveway faded to nothing. There was nobody else within miles but me and that husky young cowboy.

The Bible says that if any two touch on earth, agreeing, it shall be done in heaven. That night the two of us agreed, not only that his wife would return, but that she would come to know the Lord as I had come to know Him.

As soon as I said "amen" he reached out, kissed me on the cheek and disappeared into the pen of animals behind him. I shouted at him that I would keep on praying for the two of them. I know he heard me. But even more important, I knew God had heard me. It may take a long time, just as it took me, but that's one prayer I know God's going to answer.

You see, that's why I keep on singing: because of the rewards—the rewards of being able to touch the lives of folks no one else may ever touch.

And because of that, I can now say it's been worth it all.

Two years after Mickey and I were remarried, we were on a tour of the Midwest. Our band was with us on the bus. Mickey was driving. We had left Kim with the Rileys in Texas and were moving on after concerts in St. Louis and Omaha. On a Sunday morning we were making our way across Nebraska toward Wyoming. Mickey was at the wheel. I was asleep in my bedroom in the back of the bus when I heard his voice over the intercom.

"Hey, sleepyhead, wake up. Didn't you tell me those Nebraska Nazarenes, the ones who had written you those letters and had been praying for you, were from Sidney?"

"That's right," I said sleepily.

"Didn't you write them and tell them that some day you wanted to stop by and go to church with them?"

I was wide awake by now, realizing he was leading up

to something. "That's right," I replied.

"Well, if you want to go to church with them, you better start getting ready. We'll be there in just a few minutes. We just passed a road sign that said, 'Sidney, Nebraska, 30 miles.'"

I had just enough time to get dressed and get my hair fixed when we pulled into the little town of Sidney. Mickey found a phone booth and called ahead to the house of the Reverend and Mrs. Abke. They were just leaving for church. Excitedly, they gave us directions to the church building.

We pulled up in front of the little church in our big bus just a few minutes later. While Mickey and the band headed into town for coffee and to stretch their legs, I slipped into the building. A beaming Carolyn Abke and her husband rushed to meet me. They ushered me right to the front, hugging me all the way down the aisle like I was their sister, even though we'd never met. The announcements were just finished, and the ushers were ready to take up the offering. The Abkes insisted I come to the platform. As I took my seat beside the preacher, the Abke children, who had been rehearsing a song all week to sing during the offertory, stood up and sang. The name of the song was, incredibly—"The Years the Locusts Have Eaten."

I didn't do much talking that morning, even though they wanted me to share my testimony and sing. All I could do was stand there and weep tears of gladness—praising God for His goodness. It was a time of harvest for us all. Seeds of prayer, planted first by Grandpa Moore, watered by the faithful prayers of so many, cultivated by the tender hands of my family, pruned by hard and difficult circumstances, were harvested in abundance that morning—and are still bearing fruit.

I guess that's what that verse means after all—that precious verse Mama read to me when I was a scared little girl: "And we know that all things work together for good to them that love God, to them who are the called according to His purpose" (Romans 8:28).